The CORETTA SCOTT KING AWARDS BOOK 1970–1999

Edited by Henrietta M. Smith

AMERICAN LIBRARY ASSOCIATION
CHICAGO AND LONDON
1999

016.81
C797

Cover seal designed by Lev Mills

Photographs used with biographical sketches courtesy of the publishers or by special photographers as noted.

The paper used in this publication meets the minimum requirements of American National Standard for Information Sciences—Permanence of Paper for Printed Library Materials, ANSI Z39.48-1984. ⊚

Library of Congress Cataloging-in-Publication Data

The Coretta Scott King awards book, 1970–1999 / Henrietta M. Smith, editor.
    p.   cm.
   "Coretta Scott King Task Force, Social Responsibilities Round Table."
   Includes index.
   ISBN 0-8389-3496-X
   1. Coretta Scott King Award. 2. Children's literature, American—Afro-American authors—Bibliography. 3. Children's literature, American—Afro-American authors—Awards. 4. Afro-Americans in literature—Bibliography. I. Smith, Henrietta M. II. American Library Association. Coretta Scott King Task Force.
Z1037.A2C67   1999
[PS153.N5]
016.8108'09282'08996073—dc21   99-25046

Copyright © 1999 by the American Library Association. All rights reserved except those which may be granted by Sections 107 and 108 of the Copyright Revision Act of 1976.

Printed in the United States of America.

03 02 01 00 99   5 4 3 2 1

With gratitude, this volume is dedicated to
these visionary Founders

Glyndon Flynt Greer

Mabel McKissick

John Carroll

‽‽‽

Let us celebrate the children . . .
—*Walter Dean Myers*

University Libraries
Carnegie Mellon University
Pittsburgh PA 15213-3890

Indiana State University
Terre Haute, IN 108 3-5590

CONTENTS

PREFACE

On your hands you hold a masterpiece—prepared by dedicated children's librarians who appreciate the potential impact of this volume. The books presented within these covers are magic in the hands of our children and youth, no matter their cultural heritage.

The Coretta Scott King Awards Book, 1970–1999 chronicles the glory of accomplishment by talented writers and artists. Many of these works have changed the worlds of children and youth in America and elsewhere. Some have changed the way children's literature is taught in colleges and universities. Others have affected the curricula for reading, history, and the social sciences in early childhood programs, elementary, middle, and high schools. It is hoped that these titles have influenced reading patterns in millions of homes.

The Coretta Scott King Awards have introduced notable authors and illustrators to a diverse population of readers. The creators of these works leave a legacy of quality as they share the stories of a people that continue to struggle for a piece of the American dream.

You now have up-to-date information about the Coretta Scott King Award books. There are clear summaries of the winning titles for your own reading and for sharing with your readers, whether children or youth or in post-high school programs in children's literature. The comprehensive index covers authors, illustrators, and titles.

In 1969 the early visionaries embraced the idea of an award for African American authors and illustrators of children's books. The need was long overdue even then, and is still present today, even with the increased availability of like titles. Now, more than ever, our children of color need literature that captures them in print. They need literature that helps them to understand themselves and that validates their very being. Their friends and classmates can benefit from these titles as well. Everyone can now experience what beautiful people our children are and can become.

Henrietta Smith and her editing team have once again given us a valuable gift! Enjoy!

Barbara Jones Clark
Chair, Coretta Scott King Task Force, 1997–1999
Social Responsibilities Round Table
American Library Association

Satia Marshall Orange
Director, Office for Literacy
and Outreach Services

HISTORY

During the 1969 ALA conference in Atlantic City, N.J., school librarian Glyndon Greer introduced a book award for African American authors and illustrators of books for children. The award was supported by her colleague Mabel McKissack, as well as John Carroll, a book publisher and conference exhibitor.

Beginning in 1970, Greer almost single-handedly planned and organized the annual event which first took place at a meeting of the New Jersey Library Association. The event later took place at a location in the same city as the American Library Association's annual conference. The award was named after Coretta Scott King, honoring her "courage and determination in continuing the work for peace and brotherhood," and commemorating the "life and work" of her husband, Dr. Martin Luther King Jr. Greer personally approached publishers to sponsor children's tables, sold tickets, and made other arrangements for the event until her death in 1981.

The award was first presented in May of 1970 at the New Jersey Library Association meeting to Lillie Patterson for her timely biography, *Dr. Martin Luther King, Jr.: Man of Peace*, with an honorarium from the Johnson Publishing Company, an award sponsor to this day. The first illustrator award was mentioned in 1974 and was presented to George Ford for his illustrations for Sharon Bell Mathis' biography *Ray Charles*. The illustrator award later became an established award at the annual event.

When Glyndon Greer died, Effie Lee Morris accepted the responsibility of organizing the breakfast. Morris and Jean Coleman, then director for ALA's Office for Literacy and Outreach Services, developed the criteria for the award. Through the efforts of E. J. Josey, then an ALA Councilor, the awards committee became the Coretta Scott King Task Force of the Social Responsibilities Round Table (SRRT) in 1982. Ethel Ambrose was the first chair of the Book Awards Committee.

The winning authors and illustrators of the 1980 Coretta Scott King Awards were also the first to receive encyclopedias from Encyclopædia Britannica and World Book, a tradition that continues to this day. Book Wholesalers, Inc., has joined the Johnson Publishing Company as an author award donor. Lev Mills, chair of Atlanta (Ga.) University's Art Department, designed the seal for the Coretta Scott King Award, which was adopted in 1982.

In 1993 the task force voted to recognize works of new authors and illustrators who demonstrated significant promise. Initially called the Genesis Award, it was changed to the New Talent Award in 1998.

The new millennium will see task force members developing new strategies for increased visibility for the Coretta Scott King Award. These measures will include enhancing the Internet web site at http://www.ala.org/srrt/csking, the continuation of conference programs, the marketing of this publication, and a public awareness campaign, chaired by author Virginia Hamilton, a winner of the Coretta Scott King Award and other distinguished literary awards.

A special thanks to Effie Lee Morris, formerly the director of children's services at San Francisco Public Library, and Ethel Ambrose, formerly the director of children's services for Central Arkansas Library System, who provided more information on the history of the award than space and time allowed. Their meticulous attention to detail and archival information were invaluable to this process.

SUPPORTING STATEMENTS

HARVARD MEDICAL SCHOOL
DEPARTMENT OF PSYCHIATRY

December 1, 1998

Ms. Sandra Payne
New York Public Library
Staten Island Borough Office
5 Central Avenue
Staten Island, NY 10301

Dear Ms. Payne:

I am pleased to contribute the following comments to the "welcome" section of the *Coretta Scott King Awards Book.*

It is with pride and appreciation that I salute the thirtieth anniversary of the Coretta Scott King Awards. This publication is an elegant tribute to all of the awardees, over the past three decades, for their remarkable accomplishments. Through their work, they have contributed to the literary and cultural enrichment of young people everywhere. Prior to this awards program, stories and illustrations based on African-Americans' unique experience had for too long been neglected. Imagine the past generations of black children who did not have the opportunity to partake of the richness and beauty of their own culture delivered by this host of authors and illustrators!

Strengthened by the joy and pain of these stories, young people of this generation will be more broadly enlightened than ever before. The spirit of multiculturalism and pluralism fostered by these books reinforces our country's democratic values and affirms the equality of all citizens. It is fitting that this program honors the legacy of the Rev. Dr. Martin Luther King Jr. and the leadership of Coretta Scott King. I hope this awards program will continue to inspire writers and illustrators for many generations to come. America's young people need them!

Sincerely,

Alvin F. Poussaint, MD

THE CHILDREN'S DEFENSE FUND

I am so pleased to write this welcome to the second edition of the *Coretta Scott King Awards Book,* commemorating the thirtieth anniversary of honoring Black American authors and illustrators. One of the exciting things about these annual awards is that they are given to creators of books for children and youth.

When I was a young person, I read all the time, devouring the classics as well as books by and biographies about Black Americans. In those years before the Civil Rights Movement, one had to look diligently for books about the African American experience. It was even more difficult to find books written for Black children and teenagers. That has changed, thanks in part to organizations and groups like the Coretta Scott King Awards Book Committee of the American Library Association's Social Responsibilities Round Table and their efforts to encourage veteran and new Black authors and illustrators and to bring exemplary books to the attention of parents, teachers, librarians, scholars, community leaders, and young people.

One of the most important gifts you can give a child is the love of reading. With this key to knowledge, understanding, and self-worth, a young person carries a passport to a golden future. To all those honored in this book, I extend my thanks and my admiration for your talents and commitment to making that future possible for all our children.

Marian Wright Edelman
President
The Children's Defense Fund

Author Awards

1 9 9 9 WINNER

Johnson, Angela. *Heaven.* Simon & Schuster, 1998. 144 p.

Fourteen-year-old Marley is living a warm and happy life in the small town of Heaven, Ohio, surrounded by family and friends in an almost idyllic community while enjoying a connection to the outside world through letters from her Uncle Jack. Then, quite by accident Marley learns that her parents are really her aunt and uncle, that "Uncle Jack" is really her father, and that her mother died when she was a baby. Shattered by this discovery, Marley closes herself off from parental love and affection and begins to question every thought and belief that she had once valued. The friends and family she once held dear no longer seem to offer her strength and support. Life now becomes empty and unsure. As Marley sees it, only the wide open spaces, the farmland and the fields, seem unchanged by what she has learned—and it is in these open spaces she seeks comfort. Eventually Marley begins to understand that all families have secrets, that she can accept truths about herself without coming apart, and that real "heaven" is where love is unwavering and unconditional.

Angela Johnson's compelling first person narrative is a finely tuned vehicle for an engaging protagonist who speaks with refreshing candor. The author's fluid writing is an invitation to the reader to reach a deeper appreciation for the universal search for self-identity.

From *Heaven*

I look at Momma and want her to be mine, really mine.

I feel bruised and motherless, even when I want to go to Momma lately and tell her its okay. I just want what I used to have. But I can't. My legs won't carry me to her. I miss her.

—Angela Johnson

HONOR

Grimes, Nikki. *Jazmin's Notebook.* Dial, 1998. 102 p.

Jazmin Shelby is a bright, inquisitive fourteen-year-old who puts down her feelings and observations in a journal that provides special insight to the readers of this novel. Jazmin is a girl who had a strong family beginning that has since come apart. Her father, now dead, insisted on the "z" in the spelling of her name to reflect his love for jazz. Her mother is in the hospital, suffering from a mental illness. As the story opens Jazmin finally has a home with her older sister, CeCe. She goes through the normal teenage anxieties: worries about her appearance and fears about the future. She also handles attraction to a handsome boy who takes her interest as an invitation to rape. Most troubling of all, however, is her inability to accept her mother's illness and limitations. Jazmin's writing and growing maturity finally give her the courage to visit her mother in the hospital where she gains new hope from the changes she can observe.

A stunning combination of poetry and prose brings a special dimension to this coming-of-age novel. It is written with a sense of humor and texture that will engage its readers.

From *Jazmin's Notebook*

42nd Street Library
The library
Is no place to kneel
But this cathedral of books
feels holy.
I observe a moment of silence
at the entryway . . .
The "Quiet" signs
posted everywhere
warned me not to speak.
And why would I want to?
It looked like
all the good words
were already taken.

—Nikki Grimes

Hansen, Joyce, and Gary McGowan. *Breaking Ground, Breaking Silence: The Story of New York's African Burial Ground.* Holt, 1998. 130 p.

In 1991, the African Burial Ground in New York City was rediscovered, offering scholars and ultimately *everyone* a unique look at the lives of blacks in one section of colonial America. This volume offers young people a compelling look at the work of anthropologists, historians, and scholars as they piece together the elements of this long hidden history. The authors use the physical evidence, documents, and narratives of the time to complete as much of the picture as is currently possible.

The combined skills of a team that brought scholarly research skills, an archeological background, and outstanding writing abilities to the project have produced a historically accurate and readable text. In words and pictures, Joyce Hansen and Gary McGowan describe social conditions, ancestral traditions, and types of personal effects gleaned from the study of the remains of African Americans in a volume that closes yet another gap in the history of blacks in America.

From *Breaking Ground, Breaking Silence*

The lands were unappropriated, and though within convenient distance from the city, the locality was unattractive and desolate, so that by permission the slave population were allowed to inter their dead there . . . A place meant for outcasts, the burial ground was consecrated by the prayers to God and the ancestors. It did not matter what others thought of these people of Africa. Their strength and power would come from how they viewed themselves.

—Joyce Hansen and Gary McGowan

Johnson, Angela. *The Other Side: Shorter Poems.* Orchard, 1998. 60 p.

When writer Angela Johnson received word from her grandmother that Shorter, Alabama, was about to be razed to make room for a dog track, she made a literal and mental pilgrimage there. The result of that is this captivating collection of poems. Life in the small town of Shorter is crisply described by these concise pieces with a biographical overtone. Each poem stands on its own but together they are evocative of another time with a clear sense of place and community. Johnson does not sentimentalize the past; rather, she celebrates the people who created families and communities despite the difficulties of the times. The realities of life in the rural South are never glossed over. The emotional tone of the poems varies from pathos to humor reflecting the author's early life and coming of age in a loving supportive community.

Johnson's clever use of language paints vivid pictures that allow readers to share her love and affection for her family and their small town life. Family photographs add an additional connection for readers.

From *The Other Side: Shorter Poems*

It's hard growing up in a family that
wants you to have some talent and a little
culture.
Shorter on Saturdays was stuffed with culture.
Grandma condemned me at eight to piano lessons.
Mama just shrugged and yawned when I asked her
to get me out of it. . . .
Lessons with Miss Delta: . . .
The first lesson I cried on the piano bench the whole time . . .
The second lesson . . . we both cried. . . .

—Angela Johnson

1998 WINNER

Draper, Sharon. *Forged by Fire.* Atheneum, 1997. 151 p.

Forged by Fire is a contemporary novel that unflinchingly comes to grips with many of the problems that beset the youth of twentieth century society—broken homes, drugs, and child abuse—elements that are so much a part of a dysfunctional family.

Teenaged Gerald, whom some readers met in *Tears of a Tiger,* learns early on in his troubled life that he must grow *beyond* his years if he is to survive and protect his younger sister, Angel. Gerald and Angel's lives are stalked by tragedy: the death of Aunt Queen, the one person who truly showed them love, life with a substance abusive and seemingly unaware mother, and the cruel acts of Jordan, their mother's boyfriend. Gerald finally takes matters into his own hands when he finds that Jordan is sexually molesting Angel. For some readers, the raging fire that brings Jordan to a tragic, but not entirely regrettable, end and nearly costs Angel her life may seem symbolic of the fire that raged in Gerald's spirit. It is the fire that in the end forged together this fragile family.

From *Forged by Fire*

With the flames of fire behind them, Gerald and Angel rode
together to the music of the sirens which had decorated their
past, and would forge their future.

—Sharon Draper

HONOR

Hansen, Joyce. *I Thought My Soul Would Rise and Fly: The Diary of Patsy, a Freed Girl.* Scholastic, 1997. 202 p.

The Coretta Scott King Award jury recognized *I Thought My Soul Would Rise and Fly* for extending the story of slavery into an arena seldom discussed in books for young readers.

Twelve-year-old Patsy, a slave in the Davis household in Mars Bluff, South Carolina, learns to read and write and secretly keeps a diary of the day-to-day occurrences in the "master's" family and the family of slaves he holds in bondage. Through her diary entries, individual personalities come alive: slave Nancy, who claimed that "Missus was training her to be a fine ladies maid, not a cook"; Reverend McNeal, who started the organization that "helps men and women learn about government and voting"; the field hands, who fertilize the cotton fields with pine straw . . . for the new planting next year"; and Patsy herself, who reads from *Goody Two Shoes* and secretly passes her knowledge of words and letters to the other slaves. When the Emancipation Proclamation is announced, Patsy's diary dramatically reveals the trials, tribulations, quandaries, and uncertainties in its aftermath for the freed slaves. She also presents the changes it produced in the lives of the "masters" and "mistresses" whose indolence and dependency on others' labors were uprooted and makes poignantly evident their lack of survival skills.

From *I Thought My Soul Would Rise and Fly*

The agent had papers so the people could sign a sharecropping contract for this new year.

Brother Solomon said, "No, we're leaving"

Ma'am got excited, "You must sign."

Then Douglass spoke, "You didn't keep your side of the contract. We was promised land and a school. We ain't seen either one. If it wasn't for sweet little Patsy, none of our children would've learned their letters."

Friend, my soul did rise and fly. His words still sound in my ears.

—Joyce Hansen

Haskins, James. *Bayard Rustin: Behind the Scenes of the Civil Rights Movement.* Hyperion, 1997. 121 p.

Bayard Rustin, born in 1912, was a civil rights activist and organizer whose pacifist beliefs and commitment to the principles of nonviolent action inspired Martin Luther King Jr. Because Rustin did much of his work "behind the scenes," he perhaps is not as well known as the other notable people with whom he worked in virtually every major initiative in the civil rights movement. James Haskins, in this eloquent and moving biography, brings Rustin's story of courage and commitment to the attention of a new generation of readers.

Raised by his grandparents in Pennsylvania, Rustin maintained that his Quaker grandmother was the greatest influence on his life. Citing an extensive bibliography, including primary source material, Haskins masterfully integrates the story of the civil rights movement in the United States with details of Rustin's personal and professional life, often using Rustin's words. The quotes include incidents from Rustin's childhood and young adulthood, showing the development of his beliefs and commitment to issues of peace, equality, and justice.

Although Rustin served time in prison for refusing to join the military during World War II, had been a member of the Young Communist League, and was openly homosexual, his beliefs and talents in organizing made him a dynamic leader in the civil rights movement. His skill as an organizer was most powerfully effective as he planned the procedures for the 1963 March on Washington, which led to the passage of the Civil Rights Act of 1964. Haskins creates a fascinating, respectful, and inspirational portrait of a man who left a lasting legacy in the struggle for equality and justice in the United States and throughout the world.

1 9 9 7   WINNER

Myers, Walter Dean. *Slam!* Scholastic, 1996. 270 p.

From preschool through high school, both off and on the basketball court, Harlem-born Ice and Slam have been friends. Now seventeen-year-old Greg "Slam" Harris has transferred to a Bronx high school specializing in the arts. Both young men have NBA dreams and aspirations. Slam discovers that the students at his new school are serious young artists, and it becomes apparent that he must work hard to achieve good grades and personal satisfaction. It is also apparent that the basketball team, the perennially losing Panthers, could use a star player. What the Panthers don't need is a star with an attitude, especially one who is in continual conflict with the coach. In one school year Slam and Ice take separate paths. Slam embraces athletic and academic excellence while Ice accepts cash for drugs.

Myers's fast-paced novel develops a vivid flesh-and-blood portrait of young people in the Harlem community. For basketball fans, the description of moves on the court are hard to beat.

HONOR

McKissack, Patricia C., and Fredrick L. McKissack. *Rebels against Slavery: American Slave Revolts.* Scholastic, 1996. 181 p.

Patricia and Fredrick McKissack have written a most compelling narrative of those who resisted slavery in the Americas. *Rebels against Slavery* includes the stories of individuals who bravely rebelled, runaway slaves who formed maroon communities, leaders who organized insurrections, conductors on the Underground Railroad, and those who became eloquent exponents of abolition. While the authors describe the contributions of all who fought slavery, their work emphasizes the role of African Americans. As the escaped slave and abolitionist Henry Garnet noted, "Others may be our allies, but the battle is ours." In these pages, the courage of slavery's opponents is brought to life. This book brings memories of a past that helped to map the future to a new generation. The authors stated,

> As rebels for a righteous cause, they should be remembered for the terrible risks they knowingly took, the extraordinary determination they displayed and the important role they played in the abolition of slavery.

1 9 9 6 **WINNER**

Hamilton, Virginia. *Her Stories: African American Folktales, Fairy Tales and True Tales.* Ils. Leo Dillon and Diane Dillon. Scholastic, 1995. 112 p.

In this aesthetically attractive volume Virginia Hamilton has gathered a collection of stories from the African American culture in genres to fit just about everyone's literary taste and has adapted them to her own inimitable "telling voice." As the title implies, the stories focus on African American women's stories. Notes at the end of each tale provide information on background, origin, and authenticity or historical significance. The repertoire includes familiar "girls and animals" stories such as "Little Girl and Buh Rabby" and one perhaps less familiar but thematically popular in many cultures, "Marie and Redfish." Fairy tales recall European and Asian versions of "Cinderella" and "The Talking Eggs." Readers will find that Hamilton's supernatural tales really do abound with "weird, mystical and magical elements . . . and odd and eerie events in the lives of female subjects." The true tales are touching biographical sketches of courageous women whose life stories were gleaned from documents collected under government projects in the 1920s and 1930s. In their carefully detailed illustrations master artists Leo and Diane Dillon have captured the nuances of each story—from humorous to frightening to somber. *Her Stories* is a book to savor and to share.

From *Her Stories: African American Folktales, Fairy Tales and True Tales*

As for poor Annie, some say her sons found her washed ashore. They wrapped her in an ebony shroud and put her in a coal-black coffin. A hearse drawn by black horses carried her to the wharf . . . with six of her sons on each side. They were splendid in black—black spats and black top-hats, too; and each of them seven feet tall. . . . Darkness fell, with no moon shining. The coffin was placed on a black barge. Then her tall sons climbed aboard and floated out with the coffin clear to the sea . . . vanished from sight . . . forever gone.

—Virginia Hamilton

HONOR

Curtis, Christopher Paul. *The Watsons Go to Birmingham—1963.* Delacorte, 1995. 210 p.

Ten-year-old Kenny Watson narrates this funny and touching story of his family, "The Weird Watsons" of Flint, Michigan, as they are sometimes called. He relates comic stories of the escapades of his older brother, Byron, and the efforts of his strict but loving parents to keep the boys and their little sister, Joetta, out of trouble. Before long, however, Byron's pranks become more troubling, prompting Mom and Dad to plan a trip to Grandma's in Birmingham, Alabama. Here the story subtly shifts gears. As the family travels further South, they find themselves headed for a place and time in history that will change them—and the country—forever: the civil rights movement.

Christopher Paul Curtis does a masterful job of weaving comedy and tragedy in this impressive first novel. He creates memorable and realistic characters that engage the reader from beginning to end. The author manages to present both a warm family story and a tragic episode of history in a style that makes both themes clear to the reader.

From *The Watsons Go to Birmingham—1963*

He was also very wrong about there not being anything like magic powers or genies or angels. . . . Maybe they were in the way your father smiled at you even after you'd messed something up real bad. Maybe they were in the way you understood that your mother wasn't trying to make you the laughing "sock" of the whole school when she'd call you over in front of a bunch of your friends and use spit on her finger to wipe the sleep out of your eyes. . . . you had to say, "Shut up. That's my momma, we got the same germs." . . . And I'm sure there was an angel in Birmingham when Grandma Sands wrapped her little arms around all the Weird Watsons and said, "My fambly, my beautiful, beautiful, fambly."

—Christopher Paul Curtis

Williams-Garcia, Rita. *Like Sisters on the Home Front.* Dutton, 1995. 165 p.

Gayle Whitaker is fourteen and pregnant, again. This time her mother escorts her to a women's clinic where she undergoes an abortion. The tough-talking Gayle is frightened. Mama is fed up and at the end of her rope. Drawing upon an African American tradition, Mama sends Gayle and her toddler son, Jose, down South to spend time with her minister uncle, his wife, and their daughter, the straight-laced Cousin Cookie. In this quiet, antebellum home, the former site of a slave-holding plantation, Gayle meets the family matriarch, Great. This stately, near-death grandmother has a special fondness for the somewhat wayward and ignorant girl. Great sees in Gayle her own teenage behavior. It is Great who tells Gayle stories of the past that help Gayle to see that she indeed has a future.

Gayle appeared as a minor character in Williams-Garcia's first novel, *Blue Tights*. In this, her third novel, the author continues her compassionate and humorous portrait of New York City teenagers whose flawed characters are given opportunities for tremendous growth.

Woodson, Jacqueline. *From the Notebooks of Melanin Sun.* Scholastic, 1995. 141 p.

Thirteen-year-old Melanin Sun and his mother are extremely close; they have never needed anyone else. His name was even a special bond between the two of them: Melanin because that is what made him dark, and Sun because "his mom could see the sun shining through him." Things change between the two of them during that summer of Melanin's thirteenth year. Suddenly his mama has a new friend—a white woman named Kristin. Before too long his mother admits that Kristin is more than just a friend—they are lovers. Just when Melanin is coming to grips with his own sexual feelings, he must sort out new feelings toward his mother. For a while it appears that the new truth about his mother will destroy his special relationship with her. In pain, Melanin lashes out at Mama, but eventually he decides that, despite his confusion, he needs her in his life and tries to make some connection with Kristin.

Jacqueline Woodson presents a powerful, trailblazing story, reaching across barriers of race and sexual orientation. She has created a strong, honest character

---

From *From the Notebooks of Melanin Sun*

A few minutes later, heading back into the kitchen, Kristin stopped at the foot of my bed and kicked it.

"You hate me?" she asked, smiling.

I shrugged, keeping my eyes on the game. "I don't know you. . . ."

"What do you want to know?" she asked. She had her hands in the pocket of her shorts, and the way she stood—kind of like a gangly white boy—made me want to smile. I had never met a lady, besides mama, who was so . . . so *relaxed*. . . . She stood the way I was always trying to stand, sort of cool and calm and collected.

"Nothing," I said. . . .

"How long have you been," I stuttered, "you know?"

"Gay?" She smiled, and the dimple on her cheek appeared.

—Jacqueline Woodson

in Melanin Sun, whose first-person narrative draws the reader into his innermost thoughts. Woodson reminds readers that no matter how painful, the possibility of love and understanding can be found in all human relationships.

1995 WINNER

McKissack, Patricia C., and Fredrick L. McKissack. *Christmas in the Big House, Christmas in the Quarters.* Il. John Thompson. Scholastic, 1994. 68 p.

Using details that are evidence of meticulous research and text that is presented through the voice of accomplished storytellers, the authors introduce readers to the life of the master of a plantation and his family as contrasted with the life of the slaves who work this Virginia plantation. Taking place during the last Christmas before the Southern Rebellion, the precursor of the Civil War, the book presents imaged-filled descriptions of traditions, superstitions, religious observance, songs, holiday menus, and games. The authors show the contrast between the gifts and decorations easily available to the master's family and the ingenuity of the slaves who made their decorations from nature's bounty. Descriptions of the daily, seemingly endless tasks are interspersed with words from songs "'cause singing makes the time go faster."

Rumblings of unrest filter through the activities in the big house, and in the quarters there are secretive discussions among the slaves from neighboring plantations who were given passes for a short family reunion. The book closes with a portentous message:

> The way talk goin' I got a feeling we aine gon' need to run away. One day soon we gon' celebrate the Big Times in freedom.

John Thompson's dramatic paintings, the authors' historical notes, and a useful bibliography further enrich this moving story.

HONOR

Hansen, Joyce. *The Captive.* Scholastic, 1994. 195 p.

Through the voice of a master storyteller, twelve-year-old Kofi, son of an African king, describes the way a joyful Ashanti celebration turns with unbelievable immediacy into a scene of treachery, murder, capture, and slavery.

> I became a captive . . . I had lost my home, my family and even myself. I was a slave dressed in filthy loincloth. I could hardly remember what my beautiful robe looked like.

The narration covers the horrors of the slave ship, the indignity of the slave auction market, the rigorous work assigned to the young slaves, the strange and reserved relationship Kofi observes between his "master" and the master's wife. Kofi spends hours contemplating the strange movements and mumbling of words he later learns are elements of worship, and he ponders the dichotomy of those who would profess religion and still hold others in servitude.

Over the years, Kofi masters the English language and has an enthralling encounter with the able African American seaman, Paul Cuffe. Eventually, as a freed man, Kofi visits Sierra Leone, marries his early love, Ama, and raises his family in America. The well-researched novel closes on this rich promise:

I made a decision that I too [like his father Kwame, and Paul Cuffe] would fight against slavery and open my heart and home to unfortunate men and women in bondage.... The trial of my life had not been in vain.

McKissack, Patricia, and Fredrick McKissack Jr. *Black Diamond: The Story of the Negro Baseball Leagues.* Scholastic, 1994. 184 p.

This carefully researched volume tells not only the story of the Negro baseball leagues but also dispels some early myths about the "all-American" game in general. Documents were found that stated that as early as 1845 there were organized guidelines for playing the game and that the first all-star game was played before the Civil War. The main focus of the book, however, is on the story of the African American men who played the game even though rules established in 1867 eliminated the preponderance of blacks from playing with mainstream teams.

The history covers individual players, such as the noted Satchel Paige, the lesser known but very important Moses Fleetwood Walker, nicknamed "Fleet," who played for the American Association in Toledo, Ohio, and Sol White, noted amateur ball payer but more importantly a writer from whose records much history was learned. White, for instance, chronicled the history of the Cuban Giants (1887), the first professional all black team, who in a time of racial prejudice were able to play against white teams because of their name. White writes, "not one of them was white nor could they speak a word of Spanish," but calling themselves Cuban, opened the door.

The McKissacks write of the hardships these stalwart and determined ball players suffered—the lack of eating or sleeping facilities on the road, the unwritten requirement that they often play the clown to draw fans to the games, and financial inequities—any one of which could have deterred them if it had not been for the players' deep love of the game. The book includes profiles of

From *Black Diamond*

In 1895, Bud Fowler organized the Page Fence Giants. When they arrived in town, the team rode bicycles down the street to advertise a game with either a hometown club or another barnstorming team. By 1899, Fowler had put together another squad called the All-American Black Tourists. They arrived wearing full dress suits, top hats, and silk umbrellas. In spite of what they had to do to draw a crowd, the players on these teams were excellent athletes. Contrary to the way they were portrayed in newspapers and journals, black players were not clowns or mediocre competitors. They were as good as any playing the game at the time. What they were doing was making the most out of a bad situation.

—Patricia McKissack and Fredrick McKissack Jr.

many players, some of whom finally made the major leagues: Satchel Paige, Roy Campanella, and Jackie Robinson. (It is interesting to note here that the McKissacks include as a matter of interpretation that Jackie Robinson, according to research, may *not* have been the first black to sign a major league contract.) Also included are players who after years of rejection were finally entered in the Cooperstown Baseball Hall of Fame. A briefly annotated player roster gives readers a quick overview of the many personalities that sacrificed so much for a game they loved. Several black-and-white photographs give visibility to the men, their uniforms, their publicity material, and the sense of comradery they shared.

Woodson, Jacqueline. *I Hadn't Meant to Tell You This*. Delacorte, 1994. 115 p.

Despite the differences of race and class, Marie and Lena ignore the taunts of schoolmates to become best friends. Although Marie, from a middle-class African American family, seems to have little in common with poor, white Lena, the girls share a bond that means more than their differences: both girls have lost their mothers. As they share their deepest and most personal secrets, Marie is faced with the dilemma that can often confront good friends: Can she help Lena more by betraying her confidence or should she keep her promise and remain silent?

Woodson's sensitive and skillful telling of this story places important issues before the reader: friendship across races, class differences, peer pressure, and family secrets. Woodson presents no easy answers but rather an honest portrait of the importance of seeking and finding understanding in all kinds of people.

1994 WINNER

Johnson, Angela. *Toning the Sweep.* Orchard, 1993. 103 p.

Toning the Sweep, a cross-generational story, gloriously celebrates Grandma Ola's life even as that life, ravaged by cancer, is quietly slipping away. Fourteen-year-old Emily and her mother, Diane, have come to the desert to help Ola pack, bid farewell to her beloved desert, and move to spend the rest of her life with family in Cleveland. The sunshine yellow of Ola's house seems symbolic of the joy and warmth that overshadows the impending sense of loss.

Using a camcorder, Emily videotapes Ola with each of her friends. She records their laughter and the repetition of oft-told stories of people long gone. She makes a memory of their tragedies, dreams, and hopes so many times gone unfulfilled. The camera records the reason for her mother's quiet anger against the Ola that Emily loves and brings a stronger understanding to their mother-daughter relationship. As Emily listens to Ruth and David and to Aunt Martha and all the other "aunts," she becomes aware of their philosophical approach to life that makes them as relentlessly enduring as the Arizona desert they call home. And the lives are not recorded in isolation. Emily photographs the lizards, the plants, and the trees that are the natural background of this arid place.

Readers will be intrigued to learn the poignant meaning of toning the sweep and its significance in the life of Emily and her mother. Written in poetic prose and touched lightly with humor, this is an unforgettable story steeped with emotions that will linger with the reader long beyond the final page.

From *Toning the Sweep*

I left the desert and my mama when I was seventeen years old and angry. One morning I told Ola I was moving to San Francisco. She stared at me for a few seconds before she started packing me a bag of fruit for the trip.

She was as tired of fighting as I was when she put me on the Greyhound going north. When the bus took off, I pressed my face against the window and cried. Ola followed that bus for five miles down the dusty desert road. She gave me every chance to change my mind and stop the bus, but I didn't.

—Angela Johnson

HONOR

Myers, Walter Dean. *Malcolm X: By Any Means Necessary*. Il. with black-and-white photographs. Scholastic, 1993. 210 p.

The dramatic opening chapter tells of Malcolm X's deceptively quiet confrontation with the police in Harlem and introduces readers to the multifaceted life of a man who left an indelible mark on contemporary American history. Myers provides an in-depth picture of the early years of Malcolm X, born Malcolm Little. He introduces Malcolm's father, an outspoken minister and civil rights leader in the depression era. The author presents vivid pictures of Malcolm's poverty-stricken childhood after the death of his beloved father and of his mother's slow and tragic mental breakdown that resulted in the disintegration of the Little family. Myers does not gloss over Malcolm Little's academic prowess and brilliant mind, which in his youth was often used to make a flashy but less than savory living. The author describes Malcolm Little's six years of imprisonment during which he was introduced to the principles and philosophy of Islam, a factor that was a turning point in the life of the man who became Malcolm X. And this astute author does not fail to explain to young readers the meaning of "X" as explained by Malcolm X's mentor, Muslim leader Elijah Muhammad. "X" we learn signifies the eradication of the surname that slaves were given based on their master's name. It was symbolic of the irrevocable loss of the name given in Mother Africa.

The book includes sidelights of African American history relevant to the development of Malcolm X's personality, including the Marcus Garvey movement, the heroic work of the 54th Massachusetts Regiment of Civil War fame, the Anthony Burns slave case, and Malcolm X's interaction with Fidel Castro, among others.

With quiet compassion Myers discusses Malcolm X's gradual change from total hatred of the white man—and disparaging view of Martin Luther King Jr.'s nonviolent approach to racial equality—to a man who realized that there was wisdom in being willing to accept people as individuals. This awakening came after his 1964 pilgrimage to Mecca. It marked the beginning of a negative change

From *Malcolm X*

Malcolm spoke for the voiceless, for the people from whom not even some black leaders wanted to hear. He spoke for the jobless, and for the homeless. He spoke for the young men whose hard bodies, bodies that could perform miracles on inner-city basketball courts, were not wanted in America's offices. He spoke for the millions of black Americans who saw themselves as a minority in a world in which most of the inhabitants were people of color like themselves. He spoke for the men and women who had to turn too many other cheeks, had to fight off too many insults with nothing but smiles.

—Walter Dean Myers

in the relationship between Malcolm X and Elijah Muhammad, one that many feel may have led to this outspoken leader's assassination in 1965.

With consummate skill, Myers has written the story of a complex personality in tones that make this important life accessible to young adult readers. The book is further enriched with a bibliography that includes books and periodicals covering the early 1930s to the present.

Thomas, Joyce Carol. *Brown Honey in Broomwheat Tea.* Il. Floyd Cooper. HarperCollins, 1993. unp.

The poems in this outstanding collection speak in many voices: a plea for acceptance in "Cherish Me"; cautionary wariness in the title piece, "Brown Honey in Broomwheat Tea"; and the strength that is an integral part of African American heritage in "Becoming the Tea."

But like the steeping brew
The longer I stand
The stronger I stay.

Thomas's rhythmic patterns, image-filled language, and provocative themes evoke a wide range of emotions. Although perhaps particularly attuned to the African American heritage, the ideas are worthy of contemplation and reflection by readers regardless of their ethnic heritage.

1993 WINNER

McKissack, Patricia C. *The Dark-Thirty: Southern Tales of the Supernatural.* Il. Brian Pinkney. Knopf, 1992. 122 p.

Patricia McKissack has written a collection of stories made for reading aloud or for telling "at that special time when it is neither day nor night and when shapes and shadows play tricks on the mind." There is a well-balanced mix of the humorous, the ghostly, and the supernatural among the ten entries.

Readers will probably make individual choices among topics such as the story of the Pullman porter who tried to avoid the 11:59, known as the death train, but answered its call on a gloomy night; the story of the slave who took a lesson from the wasps in making a wise decision to disobey his master; or perhaps join in the fun of mastering the monster in the tale of the chicken coop. Each story is introduced with a historical note giving its foundation or origin. Brian Pinkney's scratch-board illustrations are a fitting complement to the mood of the stories.

From *The Dark-Thirty*

The Dark-Thirty: Southern Tales of the Supernatural is a collection of original stories rooted in African American history and the oral storytelling tradition. They should be shared at that special time when it is neither day nor night and when shapes and shadows play tricks on the mind. When you feel fear tingling in your toes and zinging up your spine like a closing zipper, you have experienced the delicious horror of a tale of the dark-thirty.

—Patricia C. McKissack

HONOR

McKissack, Patricia C., and Fredrick McKissack. *Sojourner Truth: Ain't I a Woman.* Scholastic, 1992. 186 p.

The McKissacks' stirring biography has captured the strength, the steadfastness, and the perseverance of a powerful woman determined to be free. There are engrossing details of Sojourner Truth's efforts to keep her family together, to save the life of her wayward son, Peter, and to escape from the deceit of two "religious" charlatans. Meticulous research documents events in Sojourner Truth's life as she traveled in places where others dared not go, speaking out against slavery and fighting for *all* women's rights at a time when this was the calling of only a select few—and these mainly men. In a slavery dispute, for example, Sojourner Truth is recorded to be the first black woman to defeat a white man in a court of law. There was rapt attention when this imposing figure, over six feet tall, spoke with moving dignity. In answer to a minister's charge that God had intended them to be subservient since they were indeed the weaker sex, Truth responded:

> I have ploughed and I have planted. And I have gathered into barns, and no man could head me . . . I have borne children and seen them sold into slavery when I cried out in a mother's grief none heard me but Jesus—and ain't I a woman.

This moving biography is enriched with interesting photographs and a very special section of brief biographical sketches of personalities, white and black, who were a part of Sojourner Truth's memorable life.

Myers, Walter Dean. *Somewhere in the Darkness.* Scholastic, 1992. 168 p.

With a strikingly significant title, Myers sets the focus of this dramatic story. Somewhere in the darkness a father is trying to establish a relationship between himself and the son he abandoned at an early age. On a dark night Crab, just escaped from prison, shows up at his teenaged son's home. He abruptly tells guardian Mama Jean that he has come to claim his son. With this, Crab and Jimmy begin a cross-country trek during which Jimmy learns *who* his father is—an escapee, a con man, a womanizer, but still a man who wants to be a father to his son. Just before Crab's death there is that moment of reconciliation and the poignancy of that moment in which Jimmy realizes he has learned from Crab the kind of father he himself wants to be.

Jimmy thought about his having a child. It seemed so far off, like something that could never happen, but somehow would. He thought about what he would do with the child if it were a boy. He wouldn't know much about getting money to buy food for him or what thing to tell him to do except to be good and not get into trouble. But he would tell him all the secrets he knew, looking right into his eyes and telling him nothing but the truth so that every time they were together they would know things about each other. That way there would be a connection . . . something that would be there even when they weren't together. He would know . . . where their souls touched and where they didn't.

Somewhere in the Darkness speaks to all who are parents and those who someday will be.

From *Somewhere in the Darkness*

"How you doing!"

The voice startled Jimmy. He turned to see a tall, thin man leaning against the wall.

"Doing okay," Jimmy said, trying to lower his voice so he would seem older.

"Your name is Little, isn't it?" the man asked.

"Yeah," Jimmy said. "Who you?"

"I'm your father," the man replied.

—Walter Dean Myers

Walter, Mildred Pitts. *Mississippi Challenge.* Bradbury, 1992. 205 p.

Mississippi Challenge is a documented study of a state whose historical treatment of African Americans is memorable for its cruelty and inhumanity. With candor, Walter traces freedom movements past and present and details the triumphs and failures of citizens who fought and died for justice: the sit-ins of the sixties, the often fatal attempts at voter registration, and the inequalities in educational expenditures, which fostered the establishment of the freedom schools.

Blended into the text on contemporary affairs is a careful study of the early history of the state, the lives of some of the leaders, and little-known facts about nineteenth-century African American political leaders. This material helps youthful readers to link the past with the present.

Black-and-white photographs and personal interviews extend the information in this historically based reference. A scholarly bibliography provides reference sources for further research.

1992 WINNER

Myers, Walter Dean. *Now Is Your Time! The African American Struggle for Freedom.* HarperCollins, 1991. 292 p.

In his first nonfiction book, Walter Dean Myers brings to audiences of all ages a memorable history of African Americans that spans over four centuries. The opening chapters share with readers an aspect of African history often omitted in most history texts—the time of high culture, noble rulers, great centers of learning, and scholars such as Ibrahima, whose knowledge brought students from all directions to learn from him. Scholarly research, personal interviews with the descendants of those captured and brought in chains to this country, and carefully selected photographs from historical collections are the foundation of a book that eloquently tells the story of African Americans who achieved in spite of hardships. Myers's prose is moving and convincing; the interviews add a sense of the contemporary. There seems to be a challenge to young readers in the very choice of the title, *Now Is Your Time!* Like Myers, may those who share this masterpiece of American history move forward strengthened by the author's words of celebration:

> I claim the darkest moments of my people and celebrate their perseverance.
> I claim the joy and the light and the music and the genius and the muscle and the glory of these I write about . . . and of the legions who have passed this way without yet having their stories told.

HONOR

Greenfield, Eloise. *Night on Neighborhood Street.* Il. Jan Spivey Gilchrist. Dial, 1991. unp.

From dusk to deep into the night these seventeen poems celebrate life in the neighborhood at that special time when work is done. Sleepovers, crying babies, church meetings, and "Fambly Time," the child fearful of the dark, and kids playing on the street corner are all depicted. Gouache paintings highlighted with pastels accompany the poetry. Greefield recognizes the many temptations toward wrong-doing that often accompany nighttime yet shows that the community can cope by uniting and offering "warmth and life" to undo the attractions of "The Seller" and others who want to harm its inhabitants. Powerful words offer comfort and solace to children with rhythms and images that soften the darkness's ability to frighten. Night becomes friend instead of nightmare.

1991 WINNER

Taylor, Mildred D. *The Road to Memphis.* Dial, 1990. 290 p.

Cassie Logan's personal courage serves her well during a dangerous trip she makes from Mississippi to Tennessee in 1941 with her brother Stacey and his friends in Stacey's new car. Out on the open highway, the four African American teenagers, far from the protection of their families and their community, face unknown hazards at every turn in the road. This gripping narrative recreates the perilous tensions of that time and place, as Cassie crosses over an invisible boundary and suddenly finds herself traveling across the unfamiliar terrain of adulthood.

HONOR

Haskins, James. *Black Dance in America: A History Through Its People.* Il. with photographs. HarperCollins, 1990. 232 p.

Brief biographical passages about individual African American dancers are chronologically arranged and connected by descriptions of the dances they invented or refined, providing an accessible overview of this distinctive art form. Haskins also provides a social and historical context by showing the ways black dance influenced and was influenced by dance in general.

Johnson, Angela. *When I Am Old with You.* Il. David Soman. Orchard, 1990. unp.

In this warm, cross-generational story, the reader meets a child and his grandfather sharing hours of comfortable enjoyment. As they play cards, go fishing, enjoy a quiet picnic, or meet with friends at a lively party, the little boy muses that these are the things they will do together when *he* is as old as his grandfather. There is a moment of nostalgic sadness when the two are looking at the family album and each sheds tears for a different reason. One of the most endearing lines in the book is the one in which the little boy, totally unaware of age differences, reflects on the idea that when he is old *with* his grandfather, they will sit each in his own rocking chair and "just talk about things." In word and picture *When I Am Old with You* speaks with simple eloquence of the innocence of childhood.

1990 WINNER

McKissack, Patricia C., and Fredrick McKissack. *A Long Hard Journey: The Story of the Pullman Porter.* Il. with photographs. Walker, 1989. 144 p.

The authors combined in-depth research from primary and secondary sources to provide an uncompromising account of the history of African Americans who worked as porters aboard George Pullman's luxury sleeping cars.

While the first generation of porters were newly freed from enslavement and grateful for work, poor working conditions and mistreatment at the hands of management led succeeding generations to unite under the leadership of A. Philip Randolph in a struggle for better pay and fair treatment. Songs, stories, first-person accounts, and numerous black-and-white photographs accompany the narrative, which is unique in content.

HONOR

Greenfield, Eloise. *Nathaniel Talking.* Il. Jan Spivey Gilchrist. Black Butterfly Children's Books, 1988. unp.

Nathaniel is nine years old and his voice is strong in this collection of eighteen poems accompanied by black-and-white illustrations. In the rhythms of blues and rap this young male voice comes through strong and buoyant. Emotions fill the corners of the poems as Nathaniel reflects and raps about his life. His pride and strength are grounded in his family and his troubles, which he faces with confidence. Nathaniel springs to life, a vibrant, funny, clear-sighted human being.

From *Nathaniel Talking*

I see my future . . .
not all the things around me . . .
I just see me
my serious man face
thinking . . .
my big Nathaniel me
moving through the world
doing good and unusual
things

—Eloise Greenfield

Hamilton, Virginia. *The Bells of Christmas.* Il. Lambert Davis. Harcourt, 1989. 59 p.

An elegant tribute to the childlike anticipation of family Christmas observances takes place in 1890 in the Bell family home located on the historic National Road near Springfield, Ohio. Told from the point of view of twelve-year-old Jason Bell, the story offers references to independence, to travel across time and space, and to the historical period. An invigorating sense of this loving African American family's continuity combines with a warm expression of noncommercialized holiday joy.

Patterson, Lillie. *Martin Luther King, Jr., and the Freedom Movement.* Il. with photographs. Facts on File, 1989. 178 p.

Expanding this famous African American's civil rights image to that of the human rights leader who won the 1964 Nobel Peace Prize, Patterson's biography offers a reliable transition between juvenile and adult book accounts of the twentieth-century freedom fighter. The biography is illustrated with black-and-white photographs, maps, and freedom songs and includes an excellent annotated listing of further reading and a brief chronology.

1989 WINNER

Myers, Walter Dean. *Fallen Angels.* Scholastic, 1988. 309 p.

Using Vietnam for the setting and U.S. teenagers as most of the characters, this landmark novel offers a logical, easy-to-follow story about the illogic of war. Seventeen-year-old Richie Perry is the African American protagonist whose medical papers don't catch up with him before he's shipped overseas. The war at home is revealed in letters the soldiers receive from friends and family; however, almost all of the episodes occur in the jungle during tedious hours of waiting, which are occasionally interrupted by minutes of sheer terror and chaos. Although author Myers never moralizes, a highly moral core is evident throughout the mesmerizing novel. Along with Richie Perry's humanity and bravery, the book's depiction of war's brutality will be remembered long after readers finish the book.

Lord, let us feel sorrow for ourselves and all the angel warriors that fall . . .

Fallen Angels
—Walter Dean Myers

HONOR

Berry, James. *A Thief in the Village and Other Stories.* Orchard, 1987. 148 p.

The short stories in *A Thief in the Village* give the reader a picturesque glimpse into the day-to-day life of the people in a Jamaican village. The vignettes, which cover a range of emotions from sad to philosophical to humorous, sing with Berry's poetic prose. Among the children that Berry is "celebrating," we meet Becky who wants a bike so that she can ride with the Wheels-and-Brake Boys. Mum says girls don't do that, but with an "all's well that ends well" finish, Becky gets a bike and her widowed Mum gets a "boyfriend." Then there is the pathos in the story of young Gustus who, during a raging hurricane, nearly loses his life trying to save the banana tree that was marked as his personal birthright—he had hoped to make money from the sale of the fruit to buy shoes. His father did not understand this concern until Gustus's near fatal accident as he returns to his storm-torn home and is felled by the tree. In the title story, a sister and brother, Nenna and Man-Man, set up

From *A Thief in the Village and Other Stories*

Boys and men sway in the warm sea, giving our animals a good Sunday scrub with bushy siroce vines. And we don't just scrub them. We get on their backs. We turn their heads to sea and give them a great swim out. Like ourselves, horses and mules love this. Like myself, they know this event means no work today. No work means it must be Sunday. And by this time even men and women who don't have work animals swarm down and make a big sea-bathing flock in the water. And the scene is Sunday wonderful! It's like a village baptism of people and animals. Not surprising, truly, we all come out of the sea feeling baptized, brighter, more cheerful, and more spirited.

—James Berry

an all-night vigil to catch the thief who has been stealing their coconuts. *A Thief in the Village* is a charming look at the people who live and work in a tropical village that is not always a paradise.

Hamilton, Virginia. *Anthony Burns: The Defeat and Triumph of a Fugitive Slave.* Knopf, 1988. 193 p.

Biography and historical fiction are interwoven in a carefully written account of Anthony Burns's 1854 Boston trial based on the controversial federal Fugitive Slave Act. Documented from primary sources, the biographical portions concerning Burns's imprisonment and trial are interspersed with innovative fictional segments reconstructing his youth as an enslaved child in Virginia. Source notes, a list of persons in the book, excerpts from the Fugitive Slave Act, and the author's comments further increase the value of this unusual illuminating book.

1988 WINNER

Taylor, Mildred D. *The Friendship.* Il. Max Ginsburg. Dial, 1987. 53 p.

In a powerful short story issued as a single volume, the four Logan children are witnesses to a frightening scene at the general store in Strawberry, Mississippi. When a respected elder in the African American community dares to call the white store owner by his first name, the elder is brutally attacked by a group of white men who are unaware of a decades-long friendship between the two. Mr. Tom Bee refuses to be cowed by the attack, however, and he continues to call out the name of the store owner even after he is lying on the ground, bleeding. Both literally and figuratively, this deeply moving story shows children a courageous model of active resistance to racism and oppression.

HONOR

De Veaux, Alexis. *An Enchanted Hair Tale.* Il. Cheryl Hanna. Harper, 1987. 40 p.

Sudan's wonderful hair—"a fan daggle of locks and lions and lagoons"—sets him apart from other kids in his neighborhood, who tease him because he is different. Upset by their cruelty, he storms away and, far from home, stumbles upon a whole family of folks with enchanted hair who help him celebrate his differences. De Veaux's rhythmic text is full of pleasing rhyme and alliteration. Her imagery brilliantly conveys the mystery and magic of Sudan's hair. The poem is enhanced and extended by Cheryl Hanna's captivating black-and-white pencil drawings.

Lester, Julius. *The Tales of Uncle Remus: The Adventures of Brer Rabbit.* Introd. by Augusta Baker. Il. Jerry Pinkney. Dial, 1987. 151 p.

A new Uncle Remus emerges from Lester's creative reshaping of forty-eight Brer Rabbit stories from African American traditions into modified, contemporary Southern-black English. Storytelling specialist Augusta Baker's introduction speaks of the importance for contemporary children to hear these tales; Lester's foreword advises telling or reading the tales in one's own language. Occasional black-and-white drawings complement the high-spirited tales, and four watercolors are reproduced in full color on double-page spreads.

1987 WINNER

Walter, Mildred Pitts. *Justin and the Best Biscuits in the World.* Lothrop, 1986. 122 p.

After the death of his father, ten-year-old Justin finds himself living in a home "surrounded" by women—his mother and his two sisters. There is constant conflict because Justin has very set ideas about what is or is not man's work. His room is always a mess, washing dishes is not on his list of masculine chores, and if he ever tries to cook anything the kitchen becomes a disaster. But Grandfather Ward comes to the rescue when he takes Justin to his home, a prosperous ranch in Missouri, where Justin learns several lessons about what it takes to be a man. These lessons include learning how to make a bed, clean the kitchen, and make prize-winning biscuits. But for Justin and all the readers there is another reward: Walter shares a history of the contributions of black cowboys and through the grandfather's narration of his family history, a lesson in the importance of knowing who you are and where you come from. A moving moment is one in which Justin learns that it is even all right for a man to cry. Grandfather explains his tears and shares this proverb:

> The brave hide their fears but share their tears. Tears bathe the soul.

Walter has written a well-paced story with several levels of historical and social information.

HONOR

Bryan, Ashley. *Lion and the Ostrich Chicks and Other African Folk Tales.* Atheneum, 1986. 87 p.

See entry on p. 68.

Hansen, Joyce. *Which Way Freedom?* Walker, 1986. 120 p.

> You born a man, not a slave—that the thing to remember. You got to learn which way freedom be. "It here first," he said, touching his own creased forehead, "in your mind."

Some 200,000 African Americans fought in the Civil War. The figure is real but too large to encompass all of their stories in a single story. By creating one fictional representative of the 200,000, Joyce Hansen brings this impersonal statistic to life.

We meet Obi as a nineteen- or twenty-year-old Union soldier, an escaped slave with a haunting memory of his mother's cries as years earlier he was torn from her arms and sold off to a different master. In a flashback, Obi relives the years he spent after this separation from his mother as one of three young slaves on a small South Carolina tobacco farm. He was sustained during his youth by a vague plan to find his mother again on one of the Sea Islands and escape with her to Mexico. As his memories of her become cloudy, he relies on the old freed slave, Buka, to help him recall her appearance and remember the bitter tears that fell on deaf ears.

With the start of the Civil War, the pressures to harvest the tobacco crop increase, and with this so do the beatings that Obi must endure. When Obi learns that the farm and its slaves are about to be sold, he enlists Buka's help to finally realize his dream of escape. On the plantation, Obi, Easter, and young Jason were always fast friends. Because of the danger they would face in the escape attempt, Obi and Easter are forced to leave young Jason behind as they follow Buka's plans for the "journey." Easter and Obi finally part, each seeking a separate way to freedom.

The reader follows Obi's tense flight until the moment that opened the book, when Obi joined the advancing Union army and was assigned to the Sixth U.S. Artillery of Colored Troops. For the first time he could call himself by the name *he* wanted, Obidiah Booker (*Obidiah* meaning "first born" and *Booker* for his faithful counselor and friend, Buka). Was this the way to freedom?

PROFILE

A Conversation with Walter Dean Myers

A review of his body of works shows Walter Dean Myers as an award-winning author for young adults who is recognized by his peers in many national and regional settings: the International Reading Association, National Council of Teachers of English, Young Adult Library Services Association of the American Library Association, and Ohio Literary Conference and a many times winner of the Coretta Scott King Award.

Contents of this interview printed with permission of Walter Dean Myers and *Horn Book Magazine.*

Why do you write "kids'" books?

When I was getting ready to write the "Great American Novel," I supported myself writing adventure stuff for men's magazines like *Argosy*. Eventually they became "girlie" magazines, so I switched to black magazines. Then I saw that the Council on Interracial Books for Children had a contest for black writers of children's books. I entered with a picture book, and I won. Later I expanded a short story into my first novel, *Fast Sam, Cool Clyde and Stuff*. I don't think, about "The Great American Novel" anymore; I find these books fulfilling.

Will you write about the Gulf War as you did about Vietnam?

Let me tell you about a great letter I got from a kid during the Persian Gulf thing. He was so intrigued with the military he'd decided to join [that] he went out to buy some military books, and one of them was *Fallen Angels*. He decided not to go.

So you won't write about the war?

No. I'm not tempted to write a book about the Gulf War because there is a fine line between writing about a subject and glorifying it.

How do you handle negative behavior in a story?

I do writing workshops for middle school students and teenagers in Jersey City, where I live. One student wrote a story about a mother using crack. I told her you can't just drop this in. You have to give background, show *why* she is taking crack. You don't put down the person but you have to put down the behavior, devalue it, explain it, but don't condone it.

Do you keep sex out of your young adult books?

I do because it's so difficult to put it in perspective in 250 pages. You have a sixteen-year-old boy who's dying to have sex with anything that holds still! If you let him do this, how do you say that this natural act is not right? How do you bring in all the social implications?

Every time I sit down to write I think of television as a value-setter. I may write about a moral kid. Good. But TV says being tough is better. The TV people know that a certain kind of value system—"cool" masculine—is what sells beer and blue jeans. I have to counter that.

How do you teach kids to write?

I try to identify the writing process for them. I bring in my contracts, the blue slips from editors. I tell them I've got two skills: *a feeling for languages acquired from reading* and *discipline*. All else can be learned. I give them structure—show them how I do it even as I do it—the outline to the finished product. . . . I show them that writing isn't magical because here's an ordinary person (me) doing it. They see me like them because my background is similar to so many of theirs.

You'd like to see more kids choose intellect as their avenue of values?

They've got no choice. For my degree I did a project in which I interviewed 500 inmates of prisons and youth homes. I quickly found out why people are in prison. They did stupid and bad things. But I couldn't figure out why so many were repeaters. Why would they go back to such horrible conditions? The answer was: lack of academics. It bothers me that we talk about reading taking you to some magic land. Nonsense! *Reading is not a luxury.* You can't *survive* without it. You read well, handle information, or you're dead meat!

What needs to change?

I don't know about education, but I do know about *attitudes,* about the history of my people. Black people before the Civil War were learning even though they worked fourteen hours in the fields. It's obvious there's nothing wrong with the people. But we need to shift the responsibility in education to the community and to the kids!

German and Swiss kids have a sense of going to school to learn. American kids go to school to be entertained, and they dare the teacher to educate them. . . . So even if the schools are lacking in some places, the solution lies with the community and the kids. That's my view for black kids.

But having said all that, I still would say: I am a reader, I am a thinker, and I am a listener. Sometimes I hear things that disturb me. I hear now a whisper that is on the wind and it says, "Despair the children." Voices rustling like dry leaves spread rumors that the children have somehow sinned, and the wind echoes, "Despair." Despair is the song and the chorus, "Despair" people are saying "for the children are gone." But the children are not gone, nor will they go, . . . Let us understand that the children are the result of what we are; they are our history; and they are what we hope to be—they are our future. If perhaps in the past our love has been too undemanding, let us sharpen it with reason—and we have reason. If our love has become too soft, let us harden it in the concrete of our ideals, but let us celebrate the children.

Celebrate the Children

Let us celebrate the children
Let us frame their smiles with rock strong hands
And spin wonders for their minds

Let us grease ashy knees with hosanna
And braid dignity into curly hair.

Let us gather the children from the streets and shadows
And from all the lonely places of the heart.

Let us warm the rain for them
And scent it with orange blossoms

Parade them through the streets
With tambourines and tabla

Let the brasses ring
In sweet astonishment

Let the gospel choir shout praises to them
And the saints of God feed them kola nuts and honey.

Then let us speak love to them,
And love again all our mortal hours
Let us celebrate the children.

From *The People Could Fly*

They say the people could fly. Say that long ago in Africa, some of the people knew magic. And they would walk up on the air like climbin up on a gate. And they flew like blackbirds over the fields. Black, shiny wings flappin against the blue up there.

Then, many of the people were captured for Slavery. The ones that could fly shed their wings. They couldn't take their wings across the water on the slave ships. Too crowded, don't you know.

The folks were full of misery, then. Got sick with the up and down of the sea. So they forgot about flyin when they could no longer breathe the sweet scent of Africa. Say the people who could fly kept their power, although they shed their wings. They kept their secret magic in the land of slavery. They looked the same as the other people from Africa who had been coming over, who had dark skin. Say you couldn't tell anymore one who could fly from one who couldn't.

—Virginia Hamilton

1986   WINNER

Hamilton, Virginia. *The People Could Fly: American Black Folktales.* Il. Leo and Diane Dillon. Knopf, 1985. 178 p.

The first comprehensive anthology of African American folklore selected and retold especially for children includes twenty-four exquisitely crafted, individually developed tales. Historical notes accompany each story and the compilation as a whole is arranged in four categories: trickster tales, tall tales, ghost and devil tales, and stories of liberation and freedom. Hamilton handles information about the Joel Chandler Harris texts with dignity, placing those versions of the traditional tales into a historical context. Her impressive use of black English from several distinct cultures also distinguishes this excellent collection of folktales.

HONOR

Hamilton, Virginia. *Junius Over Far.* Harper, 1985. 274 p.

Junius feels a strong connection between himself and his grandfather who has recently returned to his Caribbean island home. When his grandfather's letters are suddenly filled with obscure references to pirates and kidnapping, Junius convinces his father that they must rush to grandfather's aid. Shifting points of view give readers insights into the thoughts and feelings of both the teenager and his grandfather, stressing the strength of this intergenerational

African American family. Ms. Hamilton creates a rich ambiance with a lyrical use of language filled with Caribbean cadences and rhythms.

Walter, Mildred Pitts. *Trouble's Child.* Lothrop, 1985. 157 p.

Set on Blue Island, off the coast of Louisiana, *Trouble's Child* paints a picture of life both simple and complex on the island. The narration shares superstitions, customs, folklore, traditions, and the communal sorrow of an isolated people. Martha, the protagonist, who was born during a storm and is therefore a "trouble child," longs to go to the mainland to study. Her grandmother, Titay, island matriarch and revered midwife, expects Martha to remain on the island and learn from her the secrets of healing herbs and signs. While the folks on the island watch for Martha to bring out her quilting pattern, a signal that she is ready to marry, the stalwart young woman's life is changed. Harold Saunders, an "outsider" washed ashore during a storm, and Ms Boudreaux, her teacher, support Martha in her goal to go to school and study science so that she might more effectively help her people. This is an intriguing story, a mix of the old and the new, with a satisfying ending. Walter's use of the island dialect is readable, sensitive, and consistent.

1985 WINNER

Myers, Walter Dean. *Motown and Didi: A Love Story.* Viking, 1984. 192 p.

In a story of love, violence, despair, and hope, Myers describes the unlikely courtship of a homeless young man and an ambitious young woman confronting Harlem's drug culture. Didi's dream of attending college, getting a good job, and saving her family from poverty is shattered when she comes home to find her brother Tony high on dope. Motown lives alone in a condemned, abandoned building. His only treasures are the books he is reading at the suggestion of the "professor"—his friend and mentor and the owner of the Spirit of Life bookshop. When Didi reports her brother's pusher to the police, the pusher orders that she be hurt. It is Motown who saves her from her attackers. Though she helps Motown find a small apartment, Didi resists the possibility of a romantic attachment because the quiet young man does not seem to fit her imagined future. And Motown's experiences with foster care have hardened him against needing anyone. The leisurely pace of their growing love sets the stage for the work's fast-moving conclusion. When Tony dies of an overdose, Didi begs Motown to kill the pusher who destroyed her brother. Had Motown killed the dealer, he would have destroyed his own life as well, but this near tragedy is averted.

As the Professor and Didi rush toward the impending confrontation between Motown and the dealer, Myers asks, "What was Harlem? A place, a name, a gaudy easel of colors." It is a place where drugs kill while the police take payoffs. It is a place where the city administration responds to urban decay by demolishing buildings, leaving empty lots where people dump their garbage, and then disguising the results with painted tin window covers to make it look as though abandoned buildings are still occupied. But it is also a place where Motown and Didi find one another.

The Professor tells Motown, "We're all in the tribe from the moment that we're named until the moment that the last memory of our deeds is gone. . . . When you walk down the street and you see members of the tribe falling by the wayside, you are to understand that that's part of you falling over there."

Myers has created a beautiful novel that raises the question of whether we as individuals and our nation as a society can recognize and respond to this implied challenge.

HONOR

Boyd, Candy Dawson. *Circle of Gold.* Apple/Scholastic, 1984. 124 p.

Mattie Benson is the central character in this school and family story. There is much more to the book than a recital of the trivial concerns of a group of sixth graders. In the endearing relationship between Mattie and her twin brother Matthew, the reader sees the two children trying to cope with the death of their father and the disintegration of family life when their mother cannot deal with the loss. In Mattie's friend, Toni, one sees the value of having a reliable and steadfast friend. In Angel, whose name is indeed a misnomer, and in Charlene one observes the unhappiness and trouble that can result from misplaced loyalties. Through this cast of characters the reader experiences a theft uncovered, a mother's rehabilitation through therapy, and Mattie's discovery of her own self-worth. The "circle of gold" at one level is the pin Mattie wins for her mother in an essay contest. The larger "circle of gold" is the one Mattie discovers when she is convinced of the place she has in her mother's heart.

The gentle writing, the spoken and unspoken lessons, and the exploration of human relationships were highlights that the Coretta Scott King Award jury recognized in this talented writer's first novel.

Hamilton, Virginia. *A Little Love.* Philomel, 1984. 207 p.

Sheema has no memory of her parents: her mother died after Sheema's birth and her father disappeared soon afterwards. Her maternal grandparents have raised her with love and great caring, but as she nears graduation from the vocational high school, Sheema feels the need to seek out her father. Her knowledge that he's a sign painter who lives somewhere down South is enough to set her on a journey of exploration and discovery, so she and her boyfriend Forrest load up the station wagon and hit the road. An extraordinary story emanates from the characterization of an ordinary teenager searching for her identity, with the loving support of her friends and family.

1984 WINNER

Clifton, Lucille. *Everett Anderson's Goodbye.* Il. Ann Grifalconi. Holt, 1983. 32 p.

In *Everett Anderson's Goodbye,* Lucille Clifton has encompassed the magnitude of a death in a few gentle words of understanding and compassion. Clifton shares with very young readers the five stages of death, writing with a warmth and simplicity that transcends any lengthy conversations, serious discussion, or maudlin sentimentality. When his good father dies, Everett begs, promises, questions, and fasts while his mother quietly supports and lets him know she understands. Ann Grifalconi's expressive black-and-white sketches deepen the mood of this classic, with its memorable closing words:

> Whatever happens when people die, love doesn't stop and neither will I.

HONOR

Hamilton, Virginia. *The Magical Adventures of Pretty Pearl.* HarperCollins, 1983. 311 p.

When god child Pretty Pearl announces to her older brothers, John Henry and John de Conqueror, that she would like to try life as a mortal child, they warn her about those humans and their "winning ways" before they send her down from Mount Kenya to try life in the American South during the Reconstruction era. In the midst of a long journey through the South with a cast of characters from African and African American folklore, Pearl comes upon a clandestine self-supporting community of free blacks whose only link to the outside world is trade with Cherokee and Shawnee Indians. Living among them, Pearl discovers that her brothers were right—she is so drawn to the humans that she must eventually choose between her own immortal power and her newly emerging identity within a struggling mortal community. In a compelling African American odyssey that draws from myth, legend, and history, Hamilton brilliantly explores the relationship between mortal struggle and immortal dreams.

Haskins, James. *Lena Horne.* Coward-McCann, 1983. 160 p.

Throughout her successful career as an actress and singer, Lena Horne fought against stereotyping, segregation, and racism by refusing demeaning roles and by refusing to perform in clubs that treated African Americans unfairly. Her insistence on placing her strong principles over the call of fame and money sometimes cost her work and, in her early years in show business, often made her unpopular among both her peers and her audience. Haskins characterizes the highly visible entertainer as a tough, intelligent, and ambitious woman whose struggles for self-definition began in early childhood and continue through the present day.

Thomas, Joyce Carol. *Bright Shadow.* Avon, 1983. 125 p.

Although the writing style is simple, often poetic, the plot of this brief novel is complex. There is a sense of mysticism and the spiritual, with characters beset with strained family relationships, insane cruelty, and death. Abyssinia, called Abby for short, is a sensitive young woman in love with Carl Lee—much to her father's consternation. Many believe that she has the power to "see" things, which gives an aura of suspense to parts of the story. With a sense of relief the reader finds in the conclusion that after moments of high drama, Abby and Carl Lee will have a life together. *Bright Shadow* is a challenge to the imagination and to the reader's ability to move at times outside the real world.

Walter, Mildred Pitts. *Because We Are.* Lothrop, 1983. 192 p.

Emma Walsh, outstanding black student, is entangled in problems in the all-white school for which she was especially selected. She also found that she did not fit in when she returned to all-black Manning High. During her senior year Emma has to deal with ostracism by her peers, a confrontation with a white teacher who showed only contempt for the Manning students, rocky relationships with her divorced parents, and the usual boyfriend-girlfriend complexities.

The intended audience will easily relate to many of the situations in this fast-paced story.

From *Sweet Whispers, Brother Rush*

The first time Teresa saw Brother was the way she would think of him ever after. Tree fell head over heels for him. It was love at first sight in a wild beating of her heart that took her breath. But it was a dark Friday three weeks later when it rained, hard and wicked, before she knew Brother Rush was a ghost.

—Virginia Hamilton

1983 **WINNER**

Hamilton, Virginia. *Sweet Whispers, Brother Rush.* Philomel, 1982. 215 p.

Because her mother's work takes her far from home, fourteen-year-old Tree is often left in charge of the household and caring for her brother, Dabney. She accepts the uncertainty in her life until the day she encounters the ghost of her uncle, Brother Rush, through whom she can go back in time to her early childhood. By reliving key events in the past, Tree begins to ask questions about some of the things left unsaid in her family, so that she can begin to understand herself in the broader context of her family's history. This outstanding time-fantasy deals with the complexity of human relationships, the strength of the African American family, and the importance of understanding and acknowledging one's roots.

HONOR

Lester, Julius. *This Strange New Feeling.* Dial, 1982. 149 p.

This Strange New Feeling is a collection of three well-honed stories, each filled with drama, suspense, danger, and the creative ingenuity of slaves in an endless quest for freedom. In the first tale, Lester's lyrical prose includes touches of humor tinged with bitterness as he deftly chronicles the story of Ras and Sally, who help others escape by hiding them in bales of tobacco and finally find their own freedom in a northern city.

There is a saddening poignancy in the account of Maria who, in "Where the Sun Lives," enjoyed a few years of freedom happily married to Forrest, a free man. Forrest dies suddenly and deeply in debt. Maria is "confiscated" along

He knew that smile and the tremulous fluttering in the stomach that went with this strange new feeling of freedom.

This Strange New Feeling
—Julius Lester

with other properties that legally can be used to satisfy the lender's claims. Readers are moved by the sense of dignity with which Maria approaches the auction block and through Lester's forceful prose realize that it is only Maria's *physical self* that will be enslaved. Her spirit will be forever free because she knows "where the sun lives."

"A Christmas Love Story" is a dramatic account of an enslaved couple who make a daring escape to Philadelphia when the wife poses as a young white gentleman traveling north to receive medical attention. "He" is accompanied by his very dark skinned servant, William. Tension mounts and danger lurks at every stop along the four day journey to freedom. The incident closes with Ellen and William Craft (the "couple") having to flee to England to escape the vengeance that was an integral part of President William Fillmore's Fugitive Slave Bill.

Lester includes research sources for each of the historically based events to which this master storyteller gives such stirring life.

1982   **WINNER**

Taylor, Mildred D. *Let the Circle Be Unbroken.* Dial, 1981. 394 p.

Continuing the story begun in *Song of the Trees* (1975) and *Roll of Thunder, Hear My Cry* (1976), Mildred D. Taylor creates a sequel of epic proportions as the Logans face the impact of a racist government policy that threatens

From *Let the Circle Be Unbroken*

The registrar's office was on the first floor. We stood silently before the door leading to it, reading the lettering and giving ourselves another moment to gather our courage. Mama looked around at each of us. "Ready?" she said. We nodded, and she opened the door.

A woman sitting at a typewriter, her fingers busy at the keys, glanced up as we entered, then back at the sheaf of papers from which she was typing. We stood before her, waiting. She finished a page, pulled it from the typewriter, and took the time to separate the carbons from the original before finally looking at us again. At last she deigned to speak. "What y'all want?" she asked.

Mrs. Lee Annie told her.

The woman looked as if she had just gone hard of hearing. "What?"

"Come to register so's I can vote," Mrs. Lee Annie repeated.

—Mildred D. Taylor

their farm. They must draw on the mutual support and strength of the African American community to pull through in a time of crisis. As in previous volumes, protagonist Cassie's gradual maturation is reflected by her ever-enlarging world and ever-increasing understanding of the complexities of adulthood.

HONOR

Childress, Alice. *Rainbow Jordan.* Putnam/Coward, 1981. 123 p.

Women of four generations are portrayed as fourteen-year-old Rainbow attempts to find hope and promise in her life. Her mother was a child herself when she became a parent and is of little help to Rainbow. The mother's youth, inexperience, and lack of education led to an unstable relationship between mother and child. Instead, Rainbow's involvement with other women of differing social and economic classes helps her to find out who she is with respect to demands from a foster parent, a social worker, a boyfriend, and others. Characterizations are splendid and authentic language is used skillfully.

Hunter, Kristin. *Lou in the Limelight.* Scribner, 1981. 296 p.

Hunter's scathing chronicle of the music business is a sequel to her pioneering *Soul Brothers and Sister Lou.* The song "Lament for Jethro," about a friend killed in a police raid on Lou's brother's printing shop, has become a hit and Lou and the group have come to New York under the stewardship of their "manager," Marty Ross. Marty, determined to break up the solidarity of the group by promoting Lou at the expense of the boys, has them singing in garish, uncomfortable costumes and keeps them in virtual servitude as they live in debt while he manipulates their accounts. They have become "slaves is star-spangled costumes."

The reader recoils at their exploitation, especially when Marty gives the key to Lou's room to a well-connected friend who attempts to rape her. In Las Vegas, another member of the group, Frank, is given a line of credit to encourage his gambling, and all the young people are given cocaine and other drugs until Lou comes to realize that nothing they are being given is "free." Marty steals their copyrights by registering their songs in his own name, and the group is forced to work as an opening act for a white singer "with a pseudo-black style and enormous popularity—with white audiences." Then a promised movie deal brings the group instead to a pornographic film studio.

In the midst of their troubles, the group derives strength from Jethro's mother, "Aunt" Jerutha, who comes from home to care for them; from Ben Carroll, a U.S. attorney determined to expose whites in the music business who are taking advantage of black youth; from newly found friends who arrange for them to perform in African American communities in the South; and ultimately from the continuing love of family. And always there is the strength of the music:

> Blues was art and blues was therapy; it took gloomy situations and worked on them, turned them around and inside out and upside down until you could live with them and even laugh at them.

Their harrowing experiences do not break the young singers. Hunter uses their journey as an opportunity for self-exploration, an opportunity for Lou to begin to define herself as an African American.

Mebane, Mary E. *Mary: An Autobiography.* Viking, 1981. 242 p.

This painfully honest story of growing up in the rural South in the 1930s and 1940s chronicles the struggles of a determined and talented young woman who always felt like an outsider, even within her own family. Young Mary's distinctive personal story is set against the detailed backdrop of the ordinary and familiar day-to-day life of an African American community in rural North Carolina.

1 9 8 1   WINNER

Poitier, Sidney. *This Life.* Knopf, 1980. 374 p.

This Life is a candid, outspoken autobiography of the noted actor and film star Sidney Poitier. In describing his life both in America and his native Bahamas, Poitier recounts events that evoke in the reader feelings of laughter, anger, disbelief, and respect. At the time of his birth, Poitier's parents had left Cat Island in the Bahamas to try to make a better living. It was their hope to get back to Cat Island before Poitier's birth, but this man (who grew into a rather well-built person) was born prematurely and given little chance to survive. His fight for survival seems symbolic of Poitier's entire life.

The writer describes some of the many challenges he faced before gaining public notice. The reader has to laugh at Poitier's attempt to earn a living by parking cars after he had learned how to drive by watching what true valets did. Many an accident was the result. He writes of participating in the total destruction of a restaurant in the deep South when as members of the United States Army, some of whom happened to be African Americans, he and his comrades were refused service. He speaks of voice and speech training to try to rid him of his island accent. Poitier describes the labored, disappointment-filled steps from bit-part actor to Academy Award winner and the touch of emptiness he felt on that special-award night because at that time both of his beloved parents were dead.

The book includes his activities outside stage and screen, his marriages, his friendship and conflict with Harry Belafonte, and his work with the cause espoused by Martin Luther King Jr. *This Life* is an introspective study of a man who has lived widely and, although not always, well. For today's readers perhaps the most significant message is conveyed when Poitier speaks of the fault of many of today's parents (in this he includes himself) who give their children everything and take from them the survival skill of learning the responsibility of working for things both needed and wanted. *This Life* is a thoughtful yet well-paced study of one man's view of himself and the world around him.

HONOR

De Veaux, Alexis. *Don't Explain: A Song of Billie Holiday.* Harper, 1980. 151 p.

Alexis De Veaux's respect and admiration for the singer Billie Holiday reaches out from every page of this factual, poetically written biography. The author does not dismiss the erring ways of which the singer has been accused. Nor does she overlook the high-handed manner in which Holiday was treated by the law. The story tells of some happy days and some days of hope when her family migrated to Harlem, reaching for the "good life" in the North. As a fledgling blues singer, Holiday was likened to the late Bessie Smith; and the comparison seemed not to stop there as Holiday felt the sting of racism that allegedly led to Bessie Smith's death. De Veaux's descriptions of Holiday's bout with drugs and her mercurial career that ended with the singer strapped to a bed in a prison hospital is written with a haunting beauty that makes the Billie Holiday story a book to be remembered between anger for what might questionably be called justice and tears for talent too soon lost.

1980 WINNER

Myers, Walter Dean. *The Young Landlords.* Viking, 1979. 197 p.

When a group of Harlem teenagers complain to the landlord about the condition of a tenement apartment building on their block, he sells it to them for one dollar so that they can take responsibility for the repair and upkeep themselves. With a great deal of warmth and humor, Myers offers young readers an appealing story about a group of ordinary kids who find out first-hand that, although there are no easy solutions to tough problems, the first step toward making the world a better place to live is to work together.

HONOR

Gordy, Berry, Sr. *Movin' Up: Pop Gordy Tells His Story.* Introd. by Alex Haley. Harper, 1979. 144 p.

The father of the founder of Motown records tells his own life story, beginning with his childhood in Georgia, when his father always took him along on business transactions because he recognized the boy's shrewd mind for figures. Gordy's business skills sharpened as he grew older and continued working on the family farm. When the sale of timber stumps from his land netted him $2,600, Gordy wisely decided to travel north to Detroit to cash the check rather than to raise the suspicions of unscrupulous white neighbors. He soon sent for the rest of his family to join him up North, and within a few months he had saved enough money to open a grocery store. All eight of his children worked in the store, and each one grew to be successful. However, it was his seventh son, Berry Gordy Jr., who seemed to follow most closely in his father's footsteps when it came to business. A fascinating picture of a gentle, and remarkably humble, overachiever emerges from this extraordinary autobiography that reads like an oral history.

Greenfield, Eloise, and Lessie Jones Little. *Childtimes: A Three-Generation Memoir.* Harper, 1979. 175 p.

Three women—storytellers and writers, mothers and daughters—each speak in their own distinct voices to convey history in a personal way that is unique and memorable. Photographs from the family album combine with each woman's remembrances of her "childtimes" to produce an unforgettable personal glimpse into history. Pattie Frances Ridley Jones, born December 15, 1884, speaks through family stories as well as her own writings. She was close to the slave days and remembers her mother who worked as an unpaid maid for the family that had owned her grandmother before emancipation. Lessie Blanche Jones Little, born October 1, 1906, writes of her girlhood days and adolescence, followed by Eloise Glynn Little Greenfield's writing of North

Carolina where she was born on May 17, 1929. Each voice speaks of home, family, chores, social events, and courtship. In a direct style, deceptively simple, each woman tells of the fears and hopes, poverty and hunger, love and pride, and laughter and music during her growing up years. The text draws no conclusions for children nor forces readers to study history, but this unique and vibrant compilation has an effect that is poignant and moving. The patterns of the telling link one child to the next and all to the reader. Few books have brought the everyday life of history to readers so vividly and effectively.

Haskins, James. *Andrew Young: Young Man with a Mission.* Il. with photographs. Lothrop, 1979. 192 p.

The son of an affluent dentist in New Orleans, Andrew Young was a precocious child who started kindergarten at age three and graduated from Howard University when he was just nineteen. He became an activist in the civil rights movement as a young minister in Thomasville, Georgia, and his talents as a diplomat and organizer soon thrust him into a leadership role within the Southern Christian Leadership Conference (SCLC). In 1972 he became the first African American congressman elected from the South since the Reconstruction era, and in 1976 he was appointed by President Jimmy Carter as the United States ambassador to the United Nations. In the arena of international politics, Ambassador Young became known for his directness and for his unwavering stand for human rights, a stance that was often critical of the U.S. power structure. This straightforward biography does not shy away from the controversy that surrounded Andrew Young in his public life.

Haskins, James. *James Van DerZee: The Picture Takin' Man.* Il. with Van DerZee photographs. Dodd, 1979. 252 p.

The work of James Van DerZee was unrecognized and virtually unknown in the art world until his photographs of Harlem in the 1920s and 1930s were featured in a 1968 exhibition at the Metropolitan Museum of Art entitled "Harlem on My Mind." At the time, the photographer was eighty-three years old. Because James Van DerZee's life spanned the twentieth century, because he had been able to document in photographs only a small part of what his trained eye had seen over the years, and because very little had been written about him for either adults or children, Haskins was determined to get the full story down in print by conducting interviews and corresponding with the man himself. This engaging account, based on those interviews, creates a portrait with words of the intelligent, hard-working, and dignified man who became known for his portraits of African Americans—men, women, and children of Harlem who shared these traits with the man behind the camera.

Southerland, Ellease. *Let the Lion Eat Straw.* Scribner, 1979. 247 p.

Abeba Williams spent her early years in the nurturing care of Mamma Habbleshaw in rural North Carolina. Abeba's tranquil life was changed when her natural mother took her to New York. Abeba is a strong, sensitive character who grows from childhood to womanhood under a variety of circumstances. She survives her mother's sometimes volatile temper, the advances of an incestuous uncle, and a marriage to a man who she later learns has a history of insanity. After raising a very large family and using her musical talent as a sustaining force, Abeba dies in peace, a well-respected woman in the community.

Let the Lion Eat Straw is a moving story, written in rhythmic, poetic prose. It is the story of a truly genteel woman.

1979 WINNER

Davis, Ossie. *Escape to Freedom: A Play about Young Frederick Douglass.* Viking, 1978. 89 p.

Ossie Davis, playwright and actor, lends his artistic talent to the writing of a play that affords young readers a chance to reenact scenes from the life of abolitionist Frederick Douglass. The scenes are dramatic and forthright, withholding none of the vindictiveness of cruel slave masters, as if to forcefully demonstrate the reasons for Douglass's determination to escape to freedom. The play tells of Douglass's accomplishments as a lecturer, a newspaper editor, and a fighter for women's rights at a time when such a thing was basically unheard of. Douglass's fighting spirit is summed up in a speech made after he whipped his master in a "fair fight":

> I'm free . . . I know I'm still in bondage but I got a feeling—the most important feeling in the world—I'm free.

Freedom songs are interspersed among the scenes, and there are directions for staging. However, serious copyright limitations seemed to have been placed on the use of the script for "other than personal reading." But even in that context, this powerful minidrama is well worth reading and sharing.

HONOR

Fenner, Carol. *The Skates of Uncle Richard.* Il. Ati Forberg. Random, 1978. 46 p.

The champion star skater who once fueled the dreams of nine-year-old Marsha disappears when the ice skates she'd hoped for at Christmas turn out to be ugly, old-fashioned hockey skates that once belonged to her uncle. But the dream skater gradually returns after Marsha gets an impromptu skating lesson and a demonstration of some fancy footwork on the ice from the former owner of the skates. For readers making the transition to books divided into chapters, this is an easy-to-read transition to this format—and a story that shows how hard work and determination are essential elements to make dreams come true.

Hamilton, Virginia. *Justice and Her Brothers.* Greenwillow, 1978. 217 p.

At first eleven-year-old Justice blames the pervasive sense of eeriness enveloping her home on the fact that it's the first summer she and her older brothers have been left on their own during the day while their dad is at work and their mom is enrolled in college classes. But gradually, she, her brothers, and their young neighbor, Dorian, begin to realize that the telepathic powers they all possess are greatly heightened when they work together as a unit. To their great surprise, they also realize that Justice is genetically predestined for greatness as their leader, a fact that doesn't sit well with her older brother Thomas. The compelling, original science fiction story is rooted in the reality of small-town family life, sibling rivalry, and a young girl's transformation from a fretting, uncertain child into a confident young woman ready to face whatever challenges the future may hold.

Patterson, Lillie. *Benjamin Banneker: Genius of Early America.* Il. David Scott Brown. Abingdon, 1978. 142 p.

Born on his family's tobacco farm in Maryland on November 9, 1731, Benjamin Banneker was taught to read by his grandmother, who came the colonies as Molly Walsh, an English indentured servant. Banneker's grandfather, son of a tribal king in Senegal, and his father, a freed slave from Guinea, taught him to observe the world of plants and animals around him. In a school opened by a Quaker neighbor, Banneker learned literature, history, and mathematics.

Lillie Patterson details the impact Banneker's lifelong fascination with numbers and technology had on his neighbors and ultimately his country. He built the first clock made entirely from parts manufactured in the colonies; he calculated accurate almanacs to guide farmers, fishermen, and sailors; and, at Thomas Jefferson's suggestion, he was appointed by George Washington to help survey the new nation's capital. When Pierre L'Enfant walked out on the project and returned to France with his plans, it was Banneker's expertise and continued involvement that made possible the realization of those plans in the beautiful design of Washington, D.C.

Patterson not only makes clear that the striking beauty of the Washington, D.C., capital district is the product of this African American genius's dedication, but also she emphasizes the progressive foresight he had. Banneker's 1793 almanac outlined a plan for a U.S. Secretary of Peace to establish free schools throughout the country to work for world peace. A later almanac warned against the dangers of smoking.

Patterson gracefully combines facts with fictionalized conversations. She carefully distinguishes between fact and myth, providing enough information to dramatize history while suggesting that young readers go on to more-sophisticated accounts. Underlying both this biography and Banneker's life is the wisdom, learned from his grandmother, that "life is an adventure in learning."

Peterson, Jeanne Whitehouse. *I Have a Sister, My Sister Is Deaf.* Harper, 1977. unp.

In prose that has the rhythm of poetry, Jeanne Peterson has written a story that will speak to all who work with those who cannot hear. As a loving and patient sister, she tells the reader how a deaf person understands certain things such as the barking of a dog contrasted with the purring of a cat sitting in the person's lap. She makes note of things that bring fright to a hearing child but that do not bother the deaf child—such as a clap of thunder on a stormy night or the banging of a shutter when the wind is high. She talks of the companionship that is shared as the sisters walk through the woods: "I am the one who listens for small sounds. She is the one who watches for quick movements in the grass." The illustrations in this gentle explanatory book show a multiethnic group of children sharing in the experience of the one who has a sister who is deaf.

1978 WINNER

Greenfield, Eloise. *Africa Dream.* Il. Carole Byard. HarperCollins, 1977. unp.

At first glance, Byard's pencil sketches seem airy and dreamlike; but a closer look reveals subtle details that give a sense of reality to the far off African homeland to which a young child's imagination takes her. There is an impressive amount of historical information provided through the words and images. The illustrations of noble rulers of long ago, classic architecture, and graceful people make *Africa Dream* a book of visible pride and dignity.

HONOR

Faulkner, William J. *The Days When the Animals Talked: Black American Folktales and How They Came to Be.* Il. Troy Howell. Follett, 1977. 190 p.

Looking back on his childhood, the African American folklorist William Faulkner shares stories both real and imagined. Many of the tales derive from stories he had heard from a former slave, Simon Brown, who had come as a freed man to work for the Faulkner family. In part one, the reader encounters the hardships of slavery, the frustrating powerlessness of the men and women enslaved by masters who used these individuals as they pleased—in terms of work, sex, and aggression. These stories are told without rancor, but with the depth of feeling that stirs deep emotions in the reader.

In part two Faulkner turns his pen to a dignified telling of animal stories with important information given about the symbolic importance of Brer Rabbit and his companions. In an introduction to this section Faulkner states:

> Signs of unrest, dissatisfaction and even outright protest are easy to detect in some of the longer dramatic tales. As the animals behaved in the stories so the slaves were motivated to behave in their struggle to survive. Although weaponless and defenseless, the slaves, like the small animals could at times get the better of their powerful adversaries through cunning, careful planning and occasionally social action.

Faulkner's message blended with his marvelous storytelling style made him a natural choice for Coretta Scott King Award Honors.

Glass, Frankcina. *Marvin and Tige.* St. Martin's, 1977. 232 p.

Tige at age eleven is an illiterate African American street urchin on his own after the sudden death of his mother. He survives by his wit and his ability to steal and to "find" adequate shelter. Finally, this continuous fight for survival gets the best of him and he plans suicide. At that moment in steps Marvin, a down and out, once-upon-a-time successful business man. This unlikely interracial combination team up and begin to make life livable—two lonely people who have found solace in each other. In a little more than credible series of events, Marvin finds Tige's father who had abandoned Tige's mother before the child's birth. Marvin convinces Richard Davis that he must give his son a rightful place in his family. The bittersweet ending sees Tige established in his new home but with the ties to his friend Marvin still intact. This is a warm story with touches of humor, discussions about religious beliefs, and ideas about death and the value of education. It is the story of two people who cared about each other with a relationship unencumbered by racial differences.

Greenfield, Eloise. *Mary McLeod Bethune.* Crowell, 1977. 32 p.

This sympathetic portrayal of one of the great heroines in American history is simply told but never simplistic. Greenfield skillfully weaves into the personal history of Mary McLeod Bethune aspects of post-Civil War life in America and the trauma of segregation. This straightforward telling of Bethune's unflagging devotion to making the lives of black people better through education includes a brief introduction to some of the noted personalities with whom she worked to attain her goal—money for her educational projects. Particularly interesting is the discussion of her working relationship and warm friendship with Eleanor Roosevelt. Bethune's endless struggles to make her dreams come true are as impressive as her ability to bring African Americans together to solve problems long neglected by the establishment.

Haskins, James. *Barbara Jordan.* Il. with photographs. Dial, 1977. 215 p.

> When the Constitution of the United States was completed . . . I felt somehow that George Washington and Alexander Hamilton just left me out by mistake. But through the process of amendment, interpretation, and court decision I have finally been included in "We the people."

Former congresswoman from Texas, Barbara Jordan first came to national attention as a member of the House Judiciary Committee during the Watergate hearings in 1974. Her strongly held, eloquently expressed opinions have won her friends and enemies in political circles. James Haskins captures the complexity of Barbara Jordan and her times through the eyes of her supporters and her critics. Although this biography focuses on Jordan's life as a leading political figure in Washington, D.C., Haskins provides background information that helps readers acquire a full picture of her dynamic personality.

Barbara Jordan's eloquent speaking ability and decisive critical thinking skills were nurtured from early childhood by her maternal grandfather who encouraged her to be an independent thinker. She continued to be impressive as a speaker when she was on the debating team at Texas Southern University.

Jordan's political career was marked with defeat the first few times she sought office: 1962 when she ran for the Texas House of Representatives, and again in 1964. Jordan won her seat in the Texas House of Representatives in 1965, the first African American in the Texas House since 1883. Haskins describes Jordan's career as a member of the national House of Representatives (taking office in January 1973), her appointment to the powerful Judiciary Committee, and her influential discourse during the Watergate hearings.

Haskins has provided for young adult readers the life story of a woman whose firm belief in her country may be summed up in a statement she made at the 1976 Democratic convention:

> We cannot improve on the system of government handed down to us by the founders of the Republic, but we can find new ways to implement that system and realize our destiny.

Patterson, Lillie. *Coretta Scott King.* Garrard, 1977. 96 p.

This biography begins with the dilemma of the talented Coretta Scott of choosing between a musical career and the man she loves. She assumes the role of wife and mother during the years of the organized, nonviolent civil rights protests in the South. Beginning with the Montgomery bus boycott in 1955, when the threat of violence was nearly constant, Patterson recognizes the strength and stability Coretta Scott King brought to her family and their friends and acquaintances. The emphasis is on her self-sacrifice and dedication to family. The only time she raises her voice, writes Patterson, is after a sleepless night during which she receives 40 hate calls. The book imparts well the nonviolent attitude the Kings had to practice in their personal and private lives to stay focused on the larger goal of civil rights.

Stewart, Ruth Ann. *Portia: The Life of Portia Washington Pittman, The Daughter of Booker T. Washington.* Doubleday, 1977. 154 p.

Written with sensitive objectivity, this biography presents a clear picture of Portia Washington Pittman who lived a riches-to-almost-rags life with admirable dignity. From childhood she was aware of the stature and importance of her renowned father, Booker T. Washington; details of the famous educator's life are deftly woven into the Portia story. It is of great interest to note in this biography that in spite of Booker T. Washington's outspoken support of segregation, he sent his only daughter to northern schools and colleges where she was the only black allowed to enroll. As a young woman Portia traveled abroad to study piano under a German master musician. At the same time her father was getting financial support from wealthy white philanthropists who valued the concept on which Washington was founding Tuskegee Institute:

> Cast down your bucket where you are. . . . Cast it down in agriculture, mechanics, in commerce and domestic service and in the professions. We shall prosper as we learn to dignify and glorify common labor.

The biography recalls Portia Washington's meeting with her father's adversary, W. E. B. DuBois, dining with presidents, studying under George Washington Carver, her marriage to architect Sidney Pittman, and the birth and death of her three children. There is a frank discussion of the life and death of her favorite son, Booker, a talented musician who died a victim of drug addiction. In later life one reads of her struggle to save her father's birthplace as a historical site in Virginia.

The writer evokes a sense of melancholy as she describes Portia Pittman's slow decline into poverty following her dismissal from the faculty of Tuskegee Institute, seemingly politically motivated, her living in squalor in Washington, D.C., and finally dying at ninety in peace and dignity in a home provided for her by members of the Washington, D.C., Tuskegee Alumni Association. Well-selected black-and-white photographs give an added dimension to this well-written biography.

1977 WINNER

Haskins, James. *The Story of Stevie Wonder.* Il. with photographs. Lothrop, 1976. 126 p.

A powerful story of remarkable achievement emerges from this well-written biography of a popular singer, songwriter, and musician. Blind from birth, Steveland Morris was always encouraged by his family to explore and develop his other senses, especially his senses of touch and hearing. While he was still a toddler, his mother bought him a set of cardboard drums and a toy harmonica. Stevie's musical abilities became so well known around his community that friends and neighbors bought him a real drum set, a real harmonica, and, when he was seven years old, a second-hand piano. By the time he came to the attention of Motown a few years later, he was already an accomplished musician, and Motown called him "Little Stevie Wonder, the twelve-year-old genius." Haskins tells Stevie Wonder's story by tracing his personal as well as his musical accomplishments.

HONOR

Blake, Clarence N., and Donald F. Martin. *Quiz Book on Black America.* Houghton, 1976. 206 p.

Based on scholarly research, the book contains probing questions about the achievements and contributions of black Americans in every aspect of American life. The format of the book allows the user to concentrate on an area of special interest or to browse through questions in various subject areas: education, business, sports, the arts, and social action. The book covers a broad time line with quizzes ranging from events in the mid-nineteenth century to the time of the book's publication, fulfilling its stated purpose to "make the acquisition of knowledge a pleasurable experience."

Clifton, Lucille. *Everett Anderson's Friend.* Il. Ann Grifalconi. Holt, 1976. unp.

In a series of books, the voice of Everett Anderson has spoken to young readers through the words of a poet who understands childhood concerns. In "real boy" fashion, Everett Anderson takes a dislike to his neighbor, Maria. How could he like a girl who can beat him in racing and play ball better than he can! But when Everett Anderson loses his key and goes into Maria's apartment until his mother comes home—everything changes. Everett Anderson finds friendship in Apartment 3 A—and even learns something about food from the Hispanic culture. With bouncy verse and quick poetic sketches, Clifton, a gifted storyteller, provides young readers not only with a joyful verse but, more importantly, with a "slice of life" experience worthy of being remembered. Ann Grifalconi's illustrations capture the warmth of the author's text.

Taylor, Mildred D. *Roll of Thunder, Hear My Cry.* Dial, 1976. 276 p.

Set in rural Mississippi during the depression, this novel chronicles the lives of a strong African American family struggling to hold on to their land, as seen through the eyes of their young daughter, Cassie. In spite of hard times, economically and socially, the extended Logan family fills its household with love, security, and dignity, creating and maintaining an environment from which all family members draw the strength they need to face the rigors of everyday life in the segregated South.

1 9 7 6   WINNER

Bailey, Pearl. *Duey's Tale.* Harcourt, 1975. 59 p.

The music that was so much a part of Pearl Bailey is reflected in the poetic prose of *Duey's Tale.* In a mood of philosophical musings, Duey, a seedling from a maple tree, makes observations about life and about finding out who you really are and learns a great lesson about friendship. Duey as a seedling finds himself rudely stripped from his mother roots by a strong gust of wind. While bemoaning his loss of security, he finds adventure with a friendly log and a glass bottle. The three "companions" share pleasant moments together until the time comes for each to take its destined special place in the scheme of things—a place that is marked by change. A saddened but wiser and mature Duey, now a sturdy maple tree, concludes that being different is not so bad, what really matters is that everyone "needs a little attention, and that's why people have family and friends."

Duey's Tale must surely have left the Coretta Scott King Award jury with a warm feeling and a sense that this book would leave readers reflecting not only about the story but also about the author's philosophy of life.

HONOR

Graham, Shirley. *Julius K. Nyerere: Teacher of Africa.* Messner, 1975. 192 p.

A welcomed biography at the time of its publication, this book supports the view of President Nyerere as a dedicated, modest leader-teacher who worked to liberate Tanganyika and then Zanzibar and to join the two as the new country of Tanzania. Written for young people, the book lucidly explains Nyerere's political philosophy, which views society as an extended family and which incorporates both tradition and tribal pride into its political system. Graham's view of Nyerere is positive. The repressive policies and interparty disputes at work in Tanzania at the time are discussed, although interpreted to fit with the generally positive view of Nyerere. The author employs fictional dialogue successfully at the same time as she incorporates excerpts from Nyerere's writings.

Greenfield, Eloise. *Paul Robeson.* Il. George Ford. Crowell, 1975. 33 p.

The story of Paul Robeson is offered here to young readers in easily accessible language. Greenfield smoothly compresses Robeson's personal story with his accomplishments as athlete, stage actor, and political activist. His developing political commitment and the repressive reaction against it is objectively presented in honest, unbiased terms. The timbre, style, and impact of Robeson's musical performances is conveyed. In addition, the effort and determination that it took for young Robeson to succeed as an athlete is told in terms that children can easily understand and relate to. This impressive man's unswerving dedication to pursuing justice and opposing oppression for black and poor people is offered with obvious respect, in clear and simple terms.

Myers, Walter Dean. *Fast Sam, Cool Clyde, and Stuff.* Viking, 1975. 190 p.

When Stuff was twelve and one-half years old, his family moved to 116th Street in Harlem. Six years later, he recounts his extraordinary first year with the friends he found there. Myers's first young adult novel is a tribute to the sustaining power of friendship as young people pledge to be there for one another and to understand and care for each other. "I just hope I'll always have people to care for like that and be close to," says Stuff, who seems to be speaking for the author when he adds that he would "like to be able to teach somebody else that feeling."

Myers is frank about the problems faced on 116th Street. The reader shares the pain of Clyde's father's death in an accident, the departure of Gloria's father, Charley's self-deceptive drug abuse, and the school system's failure to support Clyde's academic aspirations. The group's sense of community helps them face these challenges, as does Stuff's ability to find absurdity in adversity.

Myers's wit is expressed in his characters' language—their funny imagery and verbal sparring—and in his talent for expressing the humorous aspects of hurtful situations. When Binky's ear is bitten off during a fight, Clyde suggests a hospital visit to have it reattached. The doctor sees the frantic young people as threatening hoodlums, and the concerned friends are jailed and asked to roll up their sleeves to see if they are junkies. The reader will laugh at the almost slapstick farce, but beneath the farce we clearly see the intolerance that confronts Stuff's crowd. When they retrieve a handbag stolen by two thieves, they are assumed to have stolen the bag and again helping people is shown as futile even though shown humorously.

The closeness of the group is especially precious when contrasted with the difficulty of open communication. Stuff's father may finally hug him when he is standing by Stuff in the face of an unjustified drug arrest, but at other times his father finds it impossible to say how much he likes his son. "I guess it's hard," Stuff observes, "for people, some people anyway, to say things like that."

By the time Stuff comes to record these memories, the neighborhood has altered, the friends have dispersed. The book, then, is about a brief moment in Stuff's life, the world in which he lived, the community that helped him confront that world, and the universal need to find such a community in our own lives.

Taylor, Mildred D. *Song of the Trees.* Dial, 1975. 48 p.

Eight-year-old Cassie Logan loves the majestic old trees on her family's property almost as much as her daddy does. When two powerful white men scheme to cut down the trees for lumber, Mr. Logan comes up with a scheme of his own to foil the trespassers. Taylor's first published children's book shows the emergence of traits that would become the author's trademark in subsequent work: excellent characterizations, a strong sense of place, and the ability to weave a great story by drawing together threads of social history, the rural South, and African American family life.

1975 WINNER

Robinson, Dorothy. *The Legend of Africania.* Il. Herbert Temple. Johnson Publishing, 1974. unp.

The Legend of Africania is a multilevel tale. Africania is a beautiful maiden living in the harmony of her African homeland and beloved by Prince Uhuru. On a fateful day Africania is bewitched by the evil, pale-skinned Takata. She is taken to another land and imprisoned until she decides to become pale like Takata, to take on the pale-faced spirit's ways. Only when she learns that this imitation is the *real* prison does she become free and united with her lover, Prince Uhuru. On one level, this story is written with the flavor of the traditional folktale. The Coretta Scott King Award jury "read into it a much more significant story—almost an allegory. It is seen as a story of slavery, of resistance to a master's domination, and as a lesson in remembering to always take pride in one's blackness."

1974 WINNER

Mathis, Sharon Bell. *Ray Charles.* Il. George Ford. Crowell, 1973. 32 p.

This simplified biography gives young readers a glimpse into the life of a talented musician who, though blind, refused to see himself as disabled. The author highlights episodes from the childhood accident that caused the blindness to Ray Charles's special education, and, finally, his triumph as a performer of international fame. In this inspirational portrayal, Ray Charles is seen not as handicapped but as *handicapable.*

HONOR

Childress, Alice. *A Hero Ain't Nothin' but a Sandwich.* Coward-McCann, 1973. 169 p.

Benjie Johnson is thirteen and "ain't a chile no more." He is a junkie, and his habit is destroying his life and ripping apart his family. From Benjie's opening words of denial, Childress introduces the principal players in Benjie's tragic story. In alternating monologues, the reader follows Benjie's story from the perspective of his family, friends, and teachers. As the perspective shifts with each succeeding chapter, Childress weaves a tapestry of authentic voices, giving life to characters through their deeds, words, and reflection in the words of others.

Drawing upon her theater background, Childress creates a novel that moves like a play — the spotlight shifting from character to character. Although the actors explain themselves to the reader, it is significant that they are not speaking to one another. One of the truths of this powerful work is the inability of the characters to communicate truthfully with each other or to see events from another's perspective. In one poignant moment, for instance, Benjie's mama wants to tell him that the "greatest thing in the world is to love someone and they love you too." Instead, this warm thought is verbalized with the mundane admonition for Benjie to brush the crumbs from his jacket!

Benjie's father has left, and his mother is ready to marry Butler Craig who lives with them. When Benjie, to support his habit, steals Butler's best clothes, Butler moves to a room downstairs. As Benjie's friend Jimmy-Lee Powell has said, "Needles divide guys," and the rift in Benjie's family seems irreparable. As Benjie flees across the roof of his building, however, Butler saves the boy from a near fall down an airshaft. Butler sees Benjie "swingin down over empty space, looking up at me, weighin' a ton and cryin' like crazy." Butler's tenuous hold on Benjie and the precipitous drop down the shaft become metaphors for their relationship and Benjie's life.

Benjie promises to report regularly to a detoxification program, and Butler will support him by meeting him there. But as the book ends, Butler is getting cold waiting for Benjie to arrive, not sure if Benjie can see him where he is standing, not sure if Benjie is late or not coming. The reader is left to interpret Butler's closing words:

> The wind is blowing colder now, but if I go in — he might get this far, then lose courage. Come on, Benjie, I believe in you.... It's nation time.... I'm waiting for you....

Clifton, Lucille. *Don't You Remember?* Il. Evaline Ness. Dutton, 1973. unp.

A familiar theme is treated with warm family love in this gentle "lap" story. Desire Mary Tate is sure that her family can "never remember anything" because her father postpones taking her to the plant where he works as an engineer, her mother doesn't bring home the "black cake with the pink letters," and not one of her big brothers will give her the promised taste of coffee! Repeating her favorite phrase of total exasperation, "Dag, double dag," Tate retreats to her room and eventually to bed. What a surprise when the next morning—after sleeping late—Tate is awakened to find that not only will she go to the plant, but because it is her birthday, she will have the black cake with pink letters *and* coffee. In simple language that is not condescending, Clifton encompasses a young child's concerns. The book invites one to read it aloud to the many little ones who feel left out and who fear that grownups do not remember those things that are terribly important in young lives.

Crane, Louise. *Ms. Africa: Profiles of Modern African Women.* Lippincott, 1973. 159 p.

This collection of biographies pays tribute to women from various geographical regions of Africa who have made significant achievements in widely diverse fields. Some of the women cited may seem familiar to contemporary readers, such as the talented singer Miriam Makeba or the often imprisoned fighter against apartheid Winnie Mandela. Included is the intriguing story of a woman engineer, with one of the longest names imaginable—a combination of her father's name, her husband's name, and her feminine name, who was in charge of managing the water supply for all residents in Madagascar. Her knowledge and ability finally gained the respect of the men she supervised. Efua Sutherland, a writer and a teacher from Ghana, is recognized as a catalyst for having authentic African stories published in many languages. Sutherland became interested in writing for children when she observed the dearth of Ghanian literature written for young audiences. As a part of this interest she studied folklore and involved groups in the dramatization of stories based on the trickster, Ananse.

Lawyers, models, political activists, civil servants, and members of the medical profession are all a part of this book about women of color who achieved in spite of racial and political odds against them.

Hunter, Kristin. *Guests in the Promised Land.* Scribner, 1973. 296 p.

Hunter speaks in the voices of young men and women in the process of defining themselves and their relationship with an often-hostile society. The stories reflect the mixed hope, anger, and destructiveness of African American young people in confrontation with a racist world.

In "Hero's Return," Jody encounters his big brother Junior, home after eighteen months "in the house" for armed robbery. Where Jody expects to find a hero with improved "connections," he instead meets a brother determined to impress upon him that jail is not the romanticized retreat of street corner fantasies.

In the tragicomedy of "BeeGee's Ghost," Freddy must arrange for a proper funeral for his dog, whose ghost is haunting the family, because the pet cemetery would not accept "colored dogs." Having buried BeeGee in the backyard, Freddy wryly notes,

> I'll never forget the night we spent with BeeGee's ghost in the kitchen. And I'll never stop wondering how some folks can hate other folks so much they'd take it out on a little dog. I bet if they knew it could come back and haunt them, though, they'd change.

In the title story "Guest in the Promised Land," Hunter's naive narrator assures us that "some people," like his friend Robert, "can't stand for anybody to be too nice to them." It was not Robert's fault that the trip arranged by white businessmen to the Cedarbrook Country Club did not work out. The young people were welcomed to play on the club grounds, but a sign on the door of the elegant dining room pointedly noted "Guests not allowed without members." When Robert entered to play the piano, his hands were snatched away from the keys while the "members" insincerely applauded his efforts. Robert expressed his bitter frustration by slashing the piano.

> I . . . knew we'd never go back there unless we could eat in the clubhouse and listen to [Robert] play, wrong notes and all. Because it ain't no Promised Land at all if some people are always guests and others are always members.

Nagenda, John. *Mukasa.* Il. Charles Lilly. Macmillan, 1973. 120 p.

In this book, based on the author's life, Nagenda's autobiography tells of a young boy in Africa who realizes the joy and importance of an education. Mukasa was born to his parents late in life and became a protected "treasure" to his mother, much to his father's chagrin. When Mukasa's father would not help raise the money to send the boy to school, the boy's creative mother found a way to do it. Through Mukasa's eyes one learns something of the educational system in his village at the time of the story and of the ingenuity of the teacher who, lacking a great supply of commercial teaching materials, creatively provided students with effective homemade learning tools. In this simple setting one gains a little insight into the activities and pranks that are a part of just about every schoolchild's experience. One might accept as a major high point of the book the closing incident when upon Mukasa's return home after graduation, his father *asks* Mukasa to teach him how to read. It was then that Mukasa decides, "Perhaps I won't be a doctor after all. Now I think I'll be a teacher."

1973 WINNER

Duckett, Alfred. *I Never Had It Made: The Autobiography of Jackie Robinson.* Putnam, 1972. 287 p.

With candor, Jackie Robinson describes the difficulties of being the first black to play in major league baseball—racially motivated problems, threats of physical violence from ball players on his and on opposing teams, and cruel criticism from several sports writers. Talent was not enough in a sport dominated by white players and white administrators.

Robinson does not try to gloss over personal problems that he and wife Rachel faced while trying to raise their children in the segregated South and in predominantly white areas in the North. The children seemingly suffered with identity problems—and for at least one—with tragic results.

In writing of his days after baseball, Robinson discusses the trials and tribulations of working in a management position for Chock-Full-O-Nuts. He also relates his attempts to work with the NAACP until what he calls "The Old Guard" forced his resignation. In conclusion this public hero explains the book's title, attesting that in spite of his success and triumphs, as a black man in a white world he *never had it made.*

1972 WINNER

Fax, Elton. *17 Black Artists.* Dodd, 1971. 306 p.

Using as a catalyst a slogan he read in Africa, "Sweet Are the Uses of Adversity," Elton Fax researched the lives of seventeen African American artists who succeeded against the odds. In each life was the intimation that recognition in the world of art was difficult—and for a black artist to know success was even more of a challenge. As an artist himself, Fax knew firsthand of the struggle to reach the top. The biographical sketches not only paint a picture of the artists as people but each one provides a picture of the social climate in which the individual lived and worked. At one point Fax provides an interesting historical note about the early portrayal of black figures as clowns and buffoons:

> Since it was not common, prior to the 1800s for artists to portray black people with seriousness and dignity, few such portrayals exist. Race chauvinism veered white artists away from such a course, and the black artist, eager for commission, dared not risk offending his white clientele.

Fax pays tribute to an early twentieth-century artist, James Herring, who in spite of skeptics established an art department at Howard University in 1921. The author writes candidly about the controversy surrounding the noted sculptor Edmonia Lewis, accused of murdering two fellow students on the campus of Oberlin College, and of the tragic life of Charlotte Amevor who struggled as a single parent. Included is a chapter on Romare Bearden who, before his death in 1988, left a legacy of illustrations for young people in *A Visit to the Country* (Harper, 1989). One learns of the background of nationally known Jacob Lawrence, whose plates for *Harriet and the Promised Land* were recently recovered and the book reissued (Simon & Schuster 1993, 1968). And one is able to read of the dauntless courage of Faith Ringgold who was the 1992 winner of the Coretta Scott King Award for illustrations in her first children's book, *Tar Beach.*

The book is a valuable volume in the annals of African American history and even more important—a valuable study of the life and work of serious artists who happen to be black.

1971 WINNER

Rollins, Charlemae. *Black Troubadour: Langston Hughes.* Rand McNally, 1970. 143 p.

Langston Hughes's poetry and prose captured the rhythms of the blues and the richness of African American speech. He created art from the full range of black experience. Charlemae Rollins met Hughes when she was children's librarian at the George C. Hall branch of the Chicago Public Library. It was during that time that Hughes was writing and discussing poetry with members of the Illinois Writers Project. A mutual interest in quality literature and in the life and concerns of African Americans led Rollins and Hughes to strike up a friendship. This friendship resulted in Rollins writing this biography for young readers.

Rollins details Hughes's childhood, spent in many far-flung places. She writes of the loving influence of Hughes's maternal grandmother, contrasting this life with the troubled visits with his father who had settled in Mexico. The author recounts Hughes's experiences as he settled down in New York's Harlem, his disappointment in the large and impersonal classes at New York University, and the segregation at Columbia University. Eventually Hughes graduated from Lincoln University in Pennsylvania while continuing to call his "beloved Harlem" home.

Rollins includes details about Hughes's relationship with Mary McLeod Bethune, at whose suggestion the poet toured the South and where—through his poetry reading concerts—he was actually able to support himself and concentrate on his writing. Rollins points out how Hughes's seemingly simple language becomes a profound comment on the America he found in his travels:

> Where is the Jim Crow section
> On this merry-go-round,
> Mister, cause I want to ride?
> Down South where I come from
> White and colored
> Can't sit side by side.
> Down South on the train
> There's a Jim Crow car.
> On the bus we're put in the back—
> But there ain't no back
> To a merry-go-round!
> Where's the horse
> For a kid that's black?

Rollins describes in some detail the breadth of Hughes's work. In the poems she cites as illustrations one is struck by the large number of now-familiar images that have entered the vernacular from his creative pen. She describes the successes and discouragements of his life, his ultimate hope, and his death in 1967.

HONOR

Angelou, Maya. *I Know Why the Caged Bird Sings.* Random, 1969. 281 p.

In this moving autobiography Maya Angelou takes the reader into the innermost depth of her personal self. With a masterful use of poetic prose, Angelou invokes moments of laughter, anger, and tears and shouts of victory for justice triumphant. The story begins when Angelou, who at that time was called Marguerite, is a youngster in Stamps, Arkansas. Here she experiences the sting of racial prejudice and of family betrayal but also the support of her wise and compassionate brother, Bailey. With a respect for the older generation, she pays tribute to her Uncle Willie from whom she learned her multiplication tables as well as many survival lessons. Angelou's early life was full of knocks and hardships, but the reader is left with a sense of having been uplifted because the author leaves a message with young readers that with fortitude, they too can overcome. There is a significant note in the closing words. Angelou has a baby out of wedlock. A solicitous aunt insists that the frightened young mother take the child into the bed with her, despite Angelou's fear that she would roll over and smother the baby. In the morning, when she finds all is well, there is this statement of strength:

> See, you don't have to think about doing the right thing. If you're for the right thing, then you do it without thinking.

With *I Know Why the Caged Bird Sings*, Maya Angelou had done "the right thing" for the Coretta Scott King Award jury.

Chisholm, Shirley. *Unbought and Unbossed.* Houghton, 1970. 177 p.

In 1968, Shirley Chisholm became the first African American woman to be elected to the U.S. House of Representatives. She writes:

> In a just and free society, it would be foolish [to gain fame for these twin attributes rather than for one's accomplishments]. I hope if I am remembered it will finally be for what I have done, not for what I happen to be. And I hope that my having made it, the hard way, can be some kind of inspiration, particularly for women.

Written shortly after the 1968 election, this work is both an autobiography and political manifesto—an exploration of Chisholm's path to Congress and her analysis of the challenges the country must meet to become "just and free." She describes in some detail her early years with relatives in Barbados, away from her parents who were struggling with the depression in Brooklyn, where she was born. She was politicized as a student at Brooklyn College, an ostensibly progressive campus rife with racism and sexism. Entering Columbia University to earn a master's degree in early childhood education, she became active in local politics. She presents a lively portrait of clubhouse politics through the success of her Unity Democratic Club in establishing a stronghold for African American candidates and the tactics she used in the state assembly to create programs to assist disadvantaged youth in college. She also worked to establish unemployment insurance for domestic workers and to preserve tenure rights for teachers whose careers were interrupted by pregnancy. Despite her refusal to accept the "traditional politics of expediency and compromise," she was elected four years later to the Ninety-first Congress on a platform emphasizing jobs, job training, educational equity, adequate housing, enforcement of antidiscrimination laws, and support for day care—a program that would be no less relevant a quarter century later.

Having led her reader through the maze of Brooklyn politics to her landmark congressional election, Representative Chisholm proceeds to offer her analysis of the most-urgent national imperatives. Though written at a very different time in our nation's history, her angry, eloquent words remain disturbingly contemporary. She traces many of the problems to the schizophrenic birth of a country that paid eloquent tribute to "liberty and justice for all" while denying full rights of citizenship to African Americans and women. To heal the "breach between . . . promises and . . . performance," Chisholm argues that we need a Congress no longer controlled by seniority and cynicism; a society in which women's rights are a reality and "women of all classes and colors" have access to effective contraception and the right to choose safe, legal, affordable abortions; a united effort by blacks to assume political power; and real equality of education for all children regardless of race or income level.

> We must join together to insist that this nation deliver on the promise it made nearly 200 years ago. . . . I feel an incredible urgency that we must do it now. If time has not run out, it is surely ominously short.

Evans, Mari. *I Am a Black Woman.* Morrow, 1970. 95 p.

Mari Evan's striking collection of poems explores the personal and political dimensions of being an African American woman. The exquisitely crafted and shaped poems affirm the black woman's experiences of love, loneliness, pain, and "a black oneness, a black strength."

Using free verse and subtle rhymes, repetitive words and phrases, and evocative imagery, Evans explores the need for love and community. In tones of sadness, anger, defiance, and hope, she reaches for freedom from an oppressive society and from self-imposed constraints. She speaks of the need for reaching out for personal relationships. She applauds those who would seize collective power. And pervading all is her celebration of her African American identity.

Graham, Lorenz. *Every Man Heart Lay Down*. Il. Colleen Browning. Crowell, 1970. unp.

When he served as ambassador to Liberia, Graham was most impressed by the rhythmic speech of the natives of that country. Listening to this kind of patois French that seemed to roll off the tongue, Graham was inspired to write a group of biblical stories using this language. One product of this endeavor was *Every Man Heart Lay Down*—a story that tells of God's plan to destroy his now evil-filled world. It is the story of his little "picayune" begging to be allowed to come into the world and save the people, a simple telling of the Christmas story when worshippers from afar come bringing gifts. Graham included the traditional gold and oil from the wise men, but in keeping with the story's setting, the "country people brought new rice . . . and every man heart lay down." *Every Man Heart Lay Down* is a timeless story written with a kind of poetic beauty and simplicity that begs to be read aloud.

Grossman, Barney, with Gladys Groom and the pupils of P.S. 150, the Bronx, New York. *Black Means* . . . Il. Charles Bible. Hill and Wang, 1970. 63 p.

Gladys Groom was the teacher and Barney Grossman the principal at P.S. 150, an elementary school in a predominantly African American and Puerto Rican neighborhood. The two adults were concerned by the many negative connotations they felt were commonly associated with blackness and began seeking positive images for their students—black, Puerto Rican, and white. They first encouraged a dialogue at home and at school with the goal of developing a "thesaurus of positive images." A close look at the student-generated products spawned the idea of putting the words in a book—a format that would reach a wider audience. The final product was the award winning *Black Means* . . .

Charles Bible's graphic drawings, strong positive black-and-white images, give dramatic visual power to this beautiful and meaningful book.

Jordan, June, and Terri Bush. *The Voice of the Children*. Holt, 1970. 101 p.

June Jordan writes,

> [Children] are the only ones always willing to make a start; they have no choice. Children are the ways the world begins again and again. But in general, our children have no voice—that we will listen to. We force, we blank them into the bugle/bell regulated lineup of the Army/school, and we insist on silence.

To give the children a voice, the author June Jordan and then junior high school teacher Terri Bush organized a creative writing workshop in the Fort Green section of Brooklyn. The children came voluntarily on Saturdays to "rap, dance, snack, browse among the books lying around, and write their stories, poems, editorials, and jokes." Out of these sessions grew a weekly magazine, *The Voice of the Children;* poetry readings; broadcasts; wider publication—and this volume of prose and poetry by twenty-five African American and Puerto Rican young people, ages nine to fifteen, whose photographs accompany June Jordan's Afterward.

Michael Goode, age twelve, writes,

> Some people talk in the hall
> Some people talk in a drawl
> Some people talk, talk, talk, talk
> And never say anything at all.

But these young people have much to say about a world gone awry. They speak of loneliness, of anger, of pain, and of the ultimate futility of hate. Vanessa Howard, age thirteen, warns ominously of

> The last scream
> The last cry of pain
> The last tear
> Last bleeding face
> Last baby drops
> Last riot
> Last of the human race.

But we are offered alternative visions as well, as in "Drums of Freedom," by Glen Thompson, age thirteen:

> Some of us will die
> but the drums will beat.
> We may even lose but,
> but the drums will beat.
> They will beat loud and strong,
>   and
>   on
>   and
>   on
> For we shall get what we want
> and the drums will beat.

Jerome Holland, age fifteen, tries to answer his own inner question in "Will I Make It?"

> I clear my throat with a slight cough,
> clear my eyes to see the way,
> hold my shoulders up high trying to
> forget the danger that might exist,
> because I'm black and wanna make it.

Peters, Margaret. *The Ebony Book of Black Achievement.* Johnson Publishing, 1970. 118 p.

As a high school teacher of English and American history, Peters was concerned about the dearth of information about African American history available to her students. She devoted her life to bringing information to the schools and to correcting distorted information. In this volume, she briefly sketches the lives of more than twenty black men and women from the fourteenth through the twentieth centuries who distinguished themselves as inventors, explorers, revolutionaries, educators, abolitionists, and business people, among other fields. Included are familiar names as well as others less frequently included in collective biographies, such as Granville Woods, whose air brake, induction telegraph, and third-rail system had a profound impact on American rail transportation. In brief sketches, Peters clearly presents her subjects' accomplishments, commitment, determination, and dedication to civilization.

Udry, Janice May. *Mary Jo's Grandmother.* Il. Eleanor Mill. Whitman, 1970. unp.

An early example of the cross-generation theme, Mary Jo visits her grandmother who lives in the country. The activities in which Mary Jo and her family participate are the gentle things that speak of unhurried and stress-free time—learning how to sew, playing with the animals on the farm, making goodies in the kitchen under Grandmother's careful guidance, and acting very responsible when Grandmother has an accident.

This book is one in a series of Mary Jo stories. It might be reasonable to surmise that the Coretta Scott King Award jury selected it as an honor book to recognize a non-black author for her sensitive treatment of a character from a minority culture.

1970 WINNER

Patterson, Lillie. *Dr. Martin Luther King, Jr.: Man of Peace.* Il. with photographs. Garrard, 1969. 27 p.

A young reader's introduction to the life of Martin Luther King Jr. and his nonviolent approach to achieving racial equality. The simply stated information and the timeliness of the book, published just after King's assassination, were among the factors that made this book the first title to receive the Coretta Scott King Award.

Illustrations from Award-winning Books

Plate 1. From *i see the rhythm*, 1999 Winner, Michele Wood.
Courtesy of Michele Wood and Children's Book Press.

Plate 2. From *The Faithful Friend*, 1996 Honor, Brian Pinkney.
Courtesy of Brian Pinkney and Simon & Schuster.

Plate 3. From *Running the Road to ABC*, 1997 Honor, Reynold Ruffins.
Courtesy of Reynold Ruffins and Simon & Schuster.

Plate 4. From *The Creation*, 1995 Winner, James Ransome.
Courtesy of James Ransome and Holiday House.

Plate 5. From *Her Stories: African American Folktales, Fairy Tales and True Tales,* 1996 Honor, Leo and Diane Dillon. Courtesy of Leo and Diane Dillon and Scholastic.

Plate 6. From *Ashley Bryan's ABC of African American Poetry,* 1998 Honor, Ashley Bryan. Courtesy of Ashley Bryan and Atheneum.

The Farmer

A plot of weeds,
an old grey mule.
Hot sun and sweat
on a bright Southern day.
Strong, stern papa
under a straw hat,
plowing and planting
his whole life away.
His backbone is forged
of African iron
and red Georgia clay.

—CAROLE BOSTON WEATHERFORD

Plate 7. From *In Daddy's Arms I Am Tall: African Americans Celebrating Fathers,* 1998 Winner, Javaka Steptoe. Courtesy of Javaka Steptoe and Lee & Low.

Plate 8. From *The Hunterman and the Crocodile: A West African Folktale,* 1998 Honor, Baba Wagué Diakité. Courtesy of Baba Wagué Diakité and Scholastic.

Plate 9. From *Meet Danitra Brown,* 1995 Honor, Floyd Cooper.
Courtesy of Floyd Cooper and Lothrop.

Plate 10. From *The Piano Man,* 1999 New Talent Award, Eric Velasquez.
Courtesy of Eric Velasquez and Walker.

Yeah,
those solos
were kickin'. Hot-buttered
bop, with lots of sassy-cool tones.
When the band did their thing, the Cotton Club
performers danced the Black Bottom, the Fish-Tail, and the Suzy-Q.
And while they were cuttin' the rug, Duke slid his honey-colored
fingertips across the ivory eighty-eights.

Plate 11.

From *Duke Ellington:
The Piano Prince and
His Orchestra,*
1999 Honor,
Brian Pinkney.
Courtesy of
Brian Pinkney
and Hyperion.

Plate 12. From *Harlem,* 1998 Honor, Christopher Myers.
Courtesy of Christopher Myers and Scholastic.

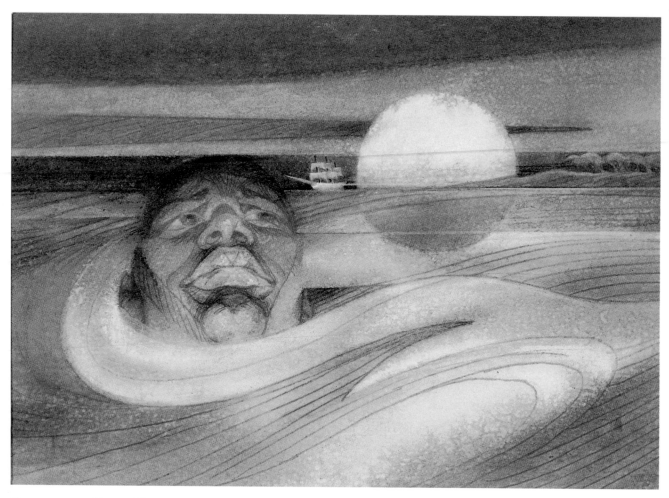

Plate 13. From *The Middle Passage: White Ships
Black Cargo*, 1996 Winner, Tom Feelings.
Courtesy of Tom Feelings and Dial.

Plate 14. From *The Palm of My Heart: Poetry by African American Children*, 1997 Honor, Gregory Christie. Courtesy of Gregory Christie and Lee & Low.

Plate 15. From *The Singing Man*, 1995 Honor, Terea Shaffer.
Courtesy of Terea Shaffer and Holiday House.

Plate 16. From *Minty: A Story of Young Harriet Tubman*, 1997 Winner, Jerry Pinkney. Courtesy of Jerry Pinkney and Dial.

Plate 17. From *The Bat Boy and His Violin*, 1999 Honor, E. B. Lewis.
Courtesy of E. B. Lewis and Simon & Schuster.

Plate 18. From *I Have Heard of a Land,* 1999 Honor, Floyd Cooper.
Courtesy of Floyd Cooper and Harper-Collins.

Plate 19. From *Neeny Coming, Neeny Going*, 1997 Honor, Synthia Saint James.
Courtesy of Synthia Saint James and BridgeWater.

Illustrator Awards

1999 WINNER

Igus, Toyomi. *i see the rhythm.* Il. **Michele Wood.** Children's Book Press, 1998.
32 p.

i see the rhythm is a multilayered history of African American music that
celebrates the far-reaching impact of this art form. The rich text includes words
from songs of various eras, definitions of musical styles, and valuable chronological time lines. Vibrant, energetic, expressionistic paintings, blended with innovative fonts and creative page design, enrich this visual chronicle of African
American music from the drum beats of Africa to stirring gospel, to the contemporary rhythms of funk, rap, and hip hop.

Wood's paintings mix a variety of styles and vivid colors to suggest musical
style and tone. The illustrator has also incorporated much historical detail in her
paintings, making them rich explorations of the text. The choice of colors and
the variety in layout make this volume a feast for the eyes and drive home in a
most dramatic fashion the importance, the depth, and the vitality of the music
forms that the work encompasses.

HONOR

Thomas, Joyce Carol. *I Have Heard of a Land.* Il. **Floyd Cooper.** Harper-
Collins, 1998. unp.

Lush double-page spread paintings heighten the sense of place in this picture depiction of the historic staged land runs of the late 1800s. It was a time
when black pioneer settlers were offered the freedom of land ownership in the
Oklahoma territory. The book especially honors the female participants who
"dared to act on their dreams." This artistic rendering presents the vastness of
the Oklahoma Territory and reflects the strength and determination of the African American pioneers.

The skillful use of light and color evokes a vivid picture of the character of
the land. The rich earth tones perfectly fit the descriptions in the text. Artist
Cooper is most successful in depicting the contrast between the great expanse
of land and the individuals who sought to tame it as well as the "connectedness"
between the land and those same individuals. With studied, but not overworked
detail, Cooper captures the challenge and spirit in the faces of the settlers he
portrays. This illustrated history will bring to life for young readers this little
known aspect of African American history.

Curtis, Gavin. *The Bat Boy and His Violin.* Il. **E. B. Lewis.** Simon & Schuster, 1998. unp.

Evocative watercolor paintings illuminate this warm family story set in the late 1940s. Music lover Reginald wants to practice his violin, but his dad, manager of the Dukes of the Negro National League, needs a bat boy. Despite the fact that Reginald is preparing for an upcoming concert, his dad insists that he accompany the team. However, Reginald finds a way while traveling with the team to pursue his first love—music—and at the same time lift the morale of the players.

E. B. Lewis's graceful watercolor paintings bring a special dimension to this unique story of intergenerational male bonding. The artist skillfully uses this technique to portray the time, the place, and the mood of the story. His careful attention to detail provides an authenticity that makes this book worthy of special attention. The almost *delicate* watercolor paintings provide an interesting backdrop to the masculinity of the baseball scenes and imply the gentle and sensitive nature of the men despite the physical nature of their game.

Pinkney, Andrea Davis. *Duke Ellington: The Piano Prince and His Orchestra.* Il. **Brian Pinkney.** Hyperion, 1998. 32 p.

Andrea Davis Pinkney's rhythmic text and artist Brian Pinkney's vibrant illustrations trace Duke Ellington's career from his childhood as a reluctant piano student to his triumphant success as a composer and orchestra leader. The swirling patterns and pulsing colors of Brian Pinkney's illustrations capture the dynamism of Duke Ellington's music. The artist uses scratchboard renderings with dyes, gouache, and paint to make the text come alive. At times, the visuals are larger than life. By figure placement on the page, Pinkney informs the reader of the important role that music played in Ellington's life. With the passage of time, Ellington's musical influence grew and expanded and the artist shows this to the reader while the author explains it in the text.

Pinkney's use of line and color bring a vibrancy to the text that reflects the feel of Ellington's music. His use of visuals and space, such as the music exploding from the instruments, right up to the "A" train seemingly *riding off the page,* will engage young readers and music lovers alike.

1998 WINNER

In Daddy's Arms I Am Tall: African Americans Celebrating Fathers. Il. **Javaka Steptoe.** Lee & Low, 1997. unp.

With imagination and creativity Javaka Steptoe designed the illustrations in this eye-intriguing volume to accompany poems from the works of several poets writing in praise of fathers and fatherhood. The designs are developed from such three-dimensional objects as buttons, chalk, pieces of window screen, paper collages, and other materials, thus giving exciting life and color to the selected poems. Steptoe discusses the variety of images:

> Each of the poems was so different, and I wanted each to have its own individuality. And so each illustration invites you to take a second look, less some innovative detail be missed.

When speaking of the art in *In Daddy's Arms I Am Tall,* Steptoe says,

> I've thought about illustrating children's books all my life . . .
> [then] I was thinking a lot about my relationships with my father and
> ideas of manhood. I thought this would be the perfect book.

The four years that it took to complete this book attest to the seriousness with which Javaka Steptoe reflected on this relationship with his father, the late great illustrator, John Steptoe.

HONOR

Ashley Bryan's ABC of African American Poetry. Il. **Ashley Bryan.** Atheneum, 1997. unp.

Vivid tempera paintings, replete with significant symbolic information, grace the pages of this oversized volume. With care and focus, Bryan has selected the works of twenty-five African and African American poets and one ever popular spiritual to introduce the youth of all cultures to the strength and beauty of these writers' words. The moods vary from poignant to humorous to those that are unforgettably thought provoking. In a masterful blend of sound and symbols, one sees and "hears" the breaking of the chains as Robert Hayden tells of Sojourner Truth walking barefoot out of slavery or God's laughter in Samuel Hayden's tribute in "Satch." Blazing firmaments, strength-filled dark eyes, love-filled brown faces of family, and the eloquent portrayal of the sturdy though time-worn face in Margaret Walker's tribute to grandmothers are just a few of the elements that said to the Coretta Scott King Award jury that this was an unforgettable collection worthy to be honored.

Diakité, Baba Wagué. *The Hunterman and the Crocodile: A West African Folktale.* Il. **Baba Wagué Diakité.** Scholastic, 1997. unp.

Bamba the crocodile and his family are on a pilgrimage to Mecca when they run out of food and water and plead with Donso the Hunterman to help them return home. After reluctantly agreeing, Donso is betrayed by Bamba, who threatens to eat him. From this beginning the reader is led into a tale of treachery—a reminder of humankind's selfish use of plants and animals. The tale underscores the importance of learning to live together in harmony.

Wagué Diakité has illustrated the storytelling with stylized, hand-painted tiles whose folkloric quality complement the text. Black figures cavort on a background of muted earth tones with subtle touches of color. The striking design of the book is evident in its interplay of decorative and representational elements, its rhythmic patterns, and its dynamic use of line. All of these features do much to extend this telling of a traditional tale. Although Wagué Diakité's work reflects his West African background, his playful illustrations are an expression of a unique artistic talent that reaches beyond all geographic boundaries.

Myers, Walter Dean. *Harlem.* Il. **Christopher Myers.** Scholastic, 1997. unp.

The community of Harlem has for decades served as a touchstone for numerous writers and visual artists. This father and son collaboration adds to that rich body of work. Christopher Myers portrays street scenes, rooftops, a church interior, the A train subway, fire escapes, nightclubs, a basketball court, living rooms, and individual people in single- and double-page spreads. His collages incorporate singular moments—hair braiding, hoop shooting, funerals, and neighbors chatting—vignettes of life in this vitality-filled community. Myers' mixed media works illuminate the poetic history of the past and the present glories of Harlem's people, their music, and their art and literature and provide a visual counterpoint to the lyrical poetry of his father. The original artwork from this oversized dynamic picture book of cultural history has been exhibited at the Studio Museum of Harlem on 125th Street.

1 9 9 7 WINNER

Schroeder, Alan. *Minty: A Story of Young Harriet Tubman.* Il. **Jerry Pinkney.** Dial, 1996. unp.

Alan Schroeder's fictionalized account of young Harriet Tubman who refused to be the "docile slave" provides the setting for Jerry Pinkney's dramatic visual interpretation of the vitality, determination, and ingenuity that marked this remarkable heroine's life. Careful research enabled this serious illustrator to depict authentic details about the dress, food, and living conditions of the plantation slaves. His own sensitivity, historical background, and passionate concern allowed Pinkney to portray in moving scenes the strength, courage, fears, and dangers young Harriet faced with unmitigated courage. Detailed watercolor spreads coupled with a master illustrator's use of space, color, and perspective provide scenes of cabin life, threatening forests, and wild-eyed fear of the would-be runaway. The artistic attention given to all aspects of the story enrich this narration that introduces young readers to an unforgettable personality later known as the Moses of her people.

HONOR

Adedjouma, Davida, ed. *The Palm of My Heart: Poetry by African American Children.* Il. **Gregory Christie.** Lee & Low, 1996. unp.

African American young people who are a part of the Inner City Youth League wrote the stirring, pride-filled words that inspired Gregory Christie's illustrations in this very special collaboration. The artist's paintings capture the joy and exultation with which the young writers see their future. His depiction of a young lady on stilts raises a proud black girl to unknown heights even as she proclaims that "Black is me—Tall, dark and wonderful." In some scenes there is a sense of spirituality, such as in the image of a church that looks down protectively on a close-knit gathering. The writers honor the elders, and Christie's art gives visual reality to the honor in a simple cross-generation painting that says, indeed, that "Black power is . . . long life."

Christie's muted paintings, like a musical accompaniment, support and interpret but never overpower the lyrical writings of the young poets.

Lauture, Denizé. *Running the Road to ABC.* Il. **Reynold Ruffins.** Simon & Schuster, 1996. unp.

Sparkling with life both in its text and its illustration, *Running the Road to ABC* imbues the reader with the joy of the desire for learning. The story, set in

Haiti, tells of six children who rise before dawn and run through the beautiful countryside on their way to school. Ruffins's magnificent, brightly colored gouache illustrations complement Lauture's poetic text. His images capture many stories of the culture—a breakfast of cornmeal, yams, and perhaps some Congo beans; book bags made from palm leaves; and the simple open-windowed schoolroom.

The pictures give one a sense of place as the illustrator uses the bright colors of the Caribbean to great effect. There is visual poetry as the paintings show first dawn in the village, stars still twinkling in the sky, the rooster sleeping while a mother bids her son good-bye on his way to ABC. From this beginning to the double-page illustration of the eager children watching attentively, paper and pencil in hand, this book sings with joy in words and pictures. In Ruffins's paintings, the reader is transported to this tropic land through pages filled with flora and fauna, frogs, snails, lizards, butterflies, donkeys, and gorgeously plumed birds. The artist's use of varying perspectives and page design, shadow and light, line and shape, create in his art endlessly fascinating illustrations.

English, Karen. *Neeny Coming, Neeny Going.* Il. **Synthia Saint James.** Bridge-
    Water, 1996. unp.

Karen English takes readers back to the 1950s, a time of change when residents of the Daufuskie Island left their homes to seek another way of life on the mainland. Young Essie awaits the return of her cousin Neeny, who was one who had left the island. Synthia Saint James has captured the bittersweet mood of Essie's excitement at the thought of Neeny's return, and the emptiness she feels because she realizes that Neeny, although physically there, has not really come back.

Flat collage-like illustrations portray life on the island: bogging for crabs, weaving baskets from sweet grass, and picking blackberries. Simple features and bright shapes show Essie running excitedly through the island to tell of Neeny's return. With this same simplicity, Saint James illustrates the fading joy and the indignation and sadness as Neeny says good-bye. Readers will find particular significance in the memory quilt Essie gives Neeny on Neeny's departure. Words and pictures in *Neeny Coming, Neeny Going* convey to the reader a culturally specific place and a part of the African American experience that has a sense of universality.

1996 WINNER

Feelings, Tom. *The Middle Passage: White Ships Black Cargo.* Il. **Tom Feelings**.
    Dial, 1995. unp.

More than thirty years ago a Ghanaian friend of Tom Feelings asked him what had happened to blacks when they were taken away from Africa to American slavery. The way to express the horror of that experience came to the artist some years later while he was living in Guyana. However, he felt he could not realize his vision without returning to the United States where he would have to confront the pain that is so much a part of the African American experience. As Feelings read about the slave trade, he saw that "callous indifference or outright brutal characterizations of Africans are embedded in the language of the Western World." He was determined to tell the story with as few words as possible. Feelings moved back to New York City where he completed the preliminary drawings in two-and-a-half years. It took almost twenty years more to revise the images so they would speak with the honesty and passion he had intended.

Feelings created a series of illustrations that eloquently describe the capture of slaves in Africa and their horrendous trip across the Atlantic to America. *The Middle Passage* opens with a sun-filled African landscape. In successive images Feelings depicts the forced march of captured slaves, the violence and claustrophobia of slave ships, and the desperate and futile attempts to escape the ships by diving into the shark-infested waters. Powerful bodies of black slaves stand out against the ghostly forms of their white tormentors. Swirling shapes echo howls of despair and yearnings for freedom.

In the introduction Feelings writes that it was while he was living in Ghana that his "drawings became more fluid and flowing. Rhythmic lines of motion, like a drumbeat, started to appear in my work, and a style that incorporated a dance consciousness surfaced." This style makes more palpable, perhaps, the horror of *The Middle Passage.* The images, executed in pen-and-ink and tempera on rice paper, are meticulously reproduced in tritone, using two black inks and one gray, plus a neutral press varnish. The care with which this oversized volume was published does honor to Feeling's work.

In completing *The Middle Passage,* Feelings expressed the hope that "those chains of the past, those shackles that physically bound us together against our wills could, in the telling, become spiritual links that willingly bind us together now and into the future."

HONOR

Hamilton, Virginia. *Her Stories: African American Folktales, Fairy Tales and True Tales.* Ils. **Leo Dillon and Diane Dillon.** Scholastic, 1995. 112 p.

The paintings that illustrate *Her Stories* capture the mood of each of these female-oriented tales with meticulous attention given to the details needed to give visual vitality to this superb collection. One cannot miss the crafty eyes in the diminutive rabbit in "Little Girl and Buh Rabby." The mermaid with stringy vine-like hair does indeed float in a jar of green water. Note how menacing the eerie cold-green, chiseled-tooth, wart-faced hag is that rides Marie's back in "Marie and the Boo Hag." By contrast, there is the quiet dignity of reality in the portraits of the women in the biographical section. The reader's eye will respond to the art of the award-winning Dillons, even as the ear responds to the words of *Her Stories.*

San Souci, Robert. *The Faithful Friend.* Il. **Brian Pinkney**. Simon & Schuster, 1995. unp.

Set in the island of Martinique, Robert San Souci's story of two faithful friends, one white and one black, is replete with those elements that are a part of the culture of the area: magic, zombies, dark forces, and romance. Brian Pinkney's specialized scratch-board technique, enriched with touches of oil paint colors, captures the changing moods of the story. Dramatic moments from the narrative come to life when the artist shows the faithful Hippolyte slowly turned to stone through the magic of the zombies. The zombies are formidable figures in their dark clothing, weaving their spells in the gloom of the tropical landscape. In contrast, the illustrator shows the delicate texture of the young bride's dress at her marriage to Clement. One can almost feel the material of the clothing of other characters. Through the drawings of the furnishings in the home, scenery in the lush tropical landscape, and small details of facial expressions and body language the illustrator displays his skill in putting into visual perspective the words of the story.

1995 **WINNER**

Johnson, James Weldon. *The Creation.* Il. **James E. Ransome.** Holiday House, 1994. unp.

A tribute to the ageless quality of James Weldon Johnson's poetic narration of the creation of the world is captured in a dramatic contemporary setting especially appropriate for today's youth. James Ransome, reflecting the power of oral tradition, portrays a wise and warm storyteller sharing the events with a rapt audience of young people. The illustrator gives life to the stirring words with shades and tones of color and the use of perspective that interprets the vastness of God's world and the move from emptiness to inhabitation. The lyrical beauty of the words is enhanced by the surrounding borders that depict the step-by-step development of the sermon until that dramatic moment when "man became a living soul," whose very physique exudes strength and purpose.

HONOR

Grimes, Nikki. *Meet Danitra Brown.* Il. **Floyd Cooper.** Lothrop, 1994. unp.

Danitra Brown is an exuberant, spunky, self-assured young person. Through Nikki Grimes's poetry Danitra expresses her "philosophy" on the importance of exposure to things of culture, how to react to those who try to "put you down," the beauty of blackness, and other important facts of life. Floyd Cooper's illustrations capture Danitra's energy in images that see her often leaping into the air, engaging in spirited dancing, and in pensive moments with a sense of life and well-being in her sparkling eyes shining through black-rimmed glasses. Cooper consistently dresses Danitra in tones of her favorite color—purple—sometimes in stripes, sometimes plaids, sometimes plain, but always purple. The illustrator symbolically uses muted tones of brown for the background as well as the skin tones of the characters in the poetry. The words and pictures reveal Danitra Brown through wise and joyful animation—"the greatest and most splendiferous girl in town."

Medearis, Angela Shelf. *The Singing Man.* Il. **Terea Shaffer.** Holiday House, 1994. unp.

The Singing Man is a folktale that lauds the importance of the griot, or praise singer, whose responsibility it is to preserve and pass on the stories of Africa's glorious history—the achievements of its rulers, artisans, and scholars. Terea Shaffer's rich oil paintings not only add drama to the story but give visualization to the diversity of the people in Nigerian regions as readers travel with the praise singer, Banzar and his teacher Sholo. The sun-baked lands over which they travel, the variations in clothing design, the facial features that distinguish one group of people from another, and the musical instruments that were used to tell the griot's stories are caught in the expressive, informative illustrations that give life to an age-old tale.

1994   WINNER

Feelings, Tom, comp. *Soul Looks Back in Wonder*. Il. **Tom Feelings.** Dial,
   1993. unp.

To convey the joy, beauty, and challenge of being African American, Tom
Feelings invited African American poets to contribute original poems to accompany his paintings. A never-before-published poem by Langston Hughes
was also included. Using a variety of techniques and mixed media, such as col-
lage, color crayon, and wallpaper, Feelings created a book that is captivating
to the eye and musical to those who listen. The artist offers striking images of
copper-colored boys and girls, children with beautiful dark faces — the youth to
whom this book was designed to inspire. In this, the artist's first book done in
color throughout, the predominant colors are the blended and textured blues,
greens, and browns of Feelings's beloved Mother Africa. Brief biographical
sketches of each of the contributing poets are included.

HONOR

Thomas, Joyce Carol. *Brown Honey in Broomwheat Tea*. Il. **Floyd Cooper.**
   HarperCollins, 1993. unp.

The striking paintings of African Americans in *Brown Honey in
Broomwheat Tea* give dramatic visualization to Joyce Carol Thomas's provocative poetry. Stirring examples of this visual feast can be seen in the strength and
dignity of the white-haired elder's face when sipping broomwheat tea, in the
artist's interpretation of the African American lineage as generations rise from
the interwoven roots of a sturdy tree, and in the trusting face of the child who
asks that "as you would cherish a thing of beauty, cherish me."

A touch of sunshine yellow illumines some part of each page — symbolic of
the light of hope that is the strength of the African American race. Cooper's art
reveals a sensitivity to Thomas's words, resulting in a book that in word and
picture is a celebration of African American life.

Mitchell, Margaree King. *Uncle Jed's Barbershop*. Il. **James Ransome.** Simon &
   Schuster, 1993. unp.

Set in the rural south, *Uncle Jed's Barbershop* is a story about holding fast
to a dream in spite of seemingly overwhelming obstacles. Uncle Jed's goal in life
was to own his own barbershop with four chairs, mirrors, sinks with running
water, and a red-and-white barber pole on the outside. Beset by the depression,
bank failures, and prejudice, Uncle Jed is forced to defer his dream. Finally, at
age 79, he opens his barbershop to the delight of all who were his "customers"
over the years.

James Ransome's paintings, full of vibrant colors, capture the moods and
extend the text of Mitchell's story. Uncle Jed is a sturdy man, cheerful and un-
defeated. He is surrounded by a warm and smiling family. The homestead is a
picture of care and neatness. One can observe the artist's care for historical ac-
curacy in the paintings of the pot-bellied stove, the crystal-set radio, the oval
rag rug — all a part of the era in which the story is set. Ransome's use of circular
lines in the rotund bodies of many of the characters, the furniture, the oval mirrors in the barbershop, and even in the round aftershave tonic bottles on the
shelf impart emotions of joy.

Ransome pays a tribute to his mentor, artist Jerry Pinkney, by including a character that resembles Pinkney among those in the picture of the people who cared about and supported Uncle Jed in his quest.

1993 WINNER

Anderson, David. *The Origin of Life on Earth. An African Creation Myth.* Il. **Kathleen Atkins Wilson.** Sights, 1991. unp.

The Origin of Life on Earth is a Yoruba legend of how the world began. Kathleen Wilson saw in the story a moving part of her own heritage. With breathtaking skill she translated the story into a visual "telling" through her distinctive style of portraying "silhouette expressions of portraits in black." As the Coretta Scott King Award jury looked at each picture there was a sense of wonderment at how many details of the text were expanded in the illustrations. There was the care of detailing the stages in the molding of each figure, the quiet respect for the shapes of the disabled—representing orisha Obatala's moment of drunken weakness. And what a contrast between the distinctive and expressive features of the silhouetted story characters and the luminous clothing in which they are garbed. Wilson's unique artistic style gives unforgettable life to a well-told story that shouts her joy and pride in her African heritage.

HONOR

Williams, Sherley Anne. *Working Cotton.* Il. **Carole Byard.** Harcourt, 1992. unp.

Double-page spreads illustrated in acrylics with mottled hues set the mood in this powerful, visual rendition of a day in the life of a black migrant family. As the day unfolds through the voice and eyes of young Shelan, Byard depicts the strength of this family through large close-up images and lush colors. The beauty of the illustrations never softens the powerful images of work and struggle that are conveyed in the text. We see the immensity of the cotton fields and the strain of hard work, yet the tenderness of the expressions reminds us of the power of love and family as the summer heat heightens weariness. It is a celebration of strength in an unjust world that makes such strength necessary to survive.

Wahl, Jan. *Little Eight John.* Il. **Wil Clay.** Lodestar, 1992. unp.

Little Eight John, a familiar character in African American folklore, is an extremely handsome young fellow but just as naughty as he is good looking. Wil Clay has captured every nuance of this mischievous child's behavior in what seem like double-vision settings. When the text speaks of one of Eight John's tricks, causing his mother to have the hiccups, the illustration gives one the illusion of movement similar to sea-sickness! When admonished not to sit backwards in the chair, the chair suddenly becomes a horse, being whipped into frenzied action by this overactive boy. Wahl's adaptation of this popular story has a happy ending, which Clay captures in the affectionate scene between a relieved mother and a repentant Little Eight John. For a visual treat, readers will enjoy the fun of examining each picture for the details that tell so much more of the story.

San Souci, Robert. *Sukey and the Mermaid.* Il. **Brian Pinkney.** Four Winds, 1992. unp.

With his scratchboard technique, Brian Pinkney has captured many subtle nuances that give an added dimension to San Souci's interpretation of this tale from the folklore of South Carolina. Using gently touches of color, Pinkney brings the figures to life in true character—the darkness of the evil father, the emerald sea colors of the mermaid, and the childlike pink in the clothing of the beleaguered young Sukey, who is abused by her greedy father. A closer look shows that the artist is also attentive to such tiny details as the part in Sukey's hair or the wisps of smoke from the father's pipe. The skillful blend of words and pictures assures the reader that *Sukey and the Mermaid* is a story to be read, to be told, and to be looked at over and over.

1992 WINNER

Ringgold, Faith. *Tar Beach.* Il. **Faith Ringgold.** Crown, 1991. unp.

Faith Ringgold is an artist. Faith Ringgold is a quilter. With her creative ingenuity, Ringgold weaves a wonderful story of hope, dreams, and dauntless courage "stitched" with the innocence of childhood. The reader meets Cassie Louise Lightfoot as she spends a hot summer evening on the roof of the apartment house—the city child's "tar beach." Looking at the sky, Cassie "flies" over a world in which her talented father will be able to work on tall buildings because, even though he is black, he will be able to join the union. She sees her family with enough income so that her hard-working mother will be able to sleep late some mornings. Then, with the mood swing that is a natural part of childhood, Cassie dreams of having ice cream for dessert *every night* because she will own the Ice Cream Factory. In all her "travels" she takes her little brother BeBe and all those who read this thoughtful picture book. The choice of colors and patterns for the material in the *Tar Beach* quilt and the arrangement of figures in the various scenes offer a three-dimensional feast for the eye and food for thought for the mind.

In addition to winning the Coretta Scott King Award, Faith Ringgold also received Caldecott honors for this, her first picture book.

HONOR

Bryan, Ashley. *All Night, All Day: A Child's First Book of African-American Spirituals.* Sel. and il. **Ashley Bryan.** Atheneum, 1991. 48 p.

More than once Ashley Bryan has voiced his concern that young African Americans and other youth are not being exposed to the melodic beauty and the historical significance of Negro spirituals. *All Night, All Day* is one of several books that this artist and scholar has designed to make the words and the music of the spirituals accessible and aesthetically pleasing to young audiences.

Bryan uses tints and shades of tempera colors to illustrate the changing moods of the twenty titles included in this collection. There is the bright yellow that glimmers in the abstract candles in "This Little Light of Mine"; swirling blues and sea greens wash around brown-hued feet in "Wade in the Water" and one cannot miss the joyous repetitious double-page spread design of the huge bells that accompany the spiritual, "Peter, Go Ring the Bells."

At the 1992 Coretta Scott King Award breakfast there was an unforgettable moment of silence when, for his acceptance "speech" for this honor book, Ashley Bryan played the title piece, "All Night, All Day" on his recorder. A book and an experience to be remembered many nights and many days.

Greenfield, Eloise. *Night on Neighborhood Street.* Il. **Jan Spivey Gilchrist.** Dial, 1991. unp.

Jan Spivey Gilchrist's use of warm shading together with blue, gold, and green colors clearly illustrate the characters portrayed in Eloise Greenfield's warm and delightful poetry. The expressions on the faces of the children and the adults and the subtle use of body language complement and enhance the author's beautiful and expressive poetry. The visual impact is further extended with the artist's use of silhouette and shading of black and white. The passage of time plays a strong role in the book. Gilchrist's use of light and shadow to denote the time of day is impressive, and such details as curtains blowing as night approaches set a mood and enhance the overall effect of the work.

There is evidence of complete communication between writer and artist as one observes how the words and the pictures evoke visual images that change with each poem. The children's faces show adoration, mischievousness, apprehension, fear, sadness, and grief in the illustrations accompanying the poems. The adults, even when captured only in shadow or silhouette, convey movement and emotion. A fine example of this is the piece "In the Church." The interaction between children and adults is well presented in such pieces as "Goodnight Juma," "Fambly Time," and "The Seller." *Night on Neighborhood Street* is a magnificent creation of mystical appearances through the use of color, light, and shading.

1991 WINNER

Price, Leontyne, adapt. *Aïda.* Ils. **Leo Dillon and Diane Dillon.** Harcourt, 1990. unp.

Upon opening the pages of *Aïda,* one stands in the entrance of a mighty palace whose marble halls invite the viewer to participate in a breathtaking artistic experience. Leo and Diane Dillon, inspired by the voice of Leontyne Price singing the title role of Aïda, knew that the diva's adaptation of this tragic opera was a book they were meant to illustrate. Each bordered full-page illustration reveals some aspect of a palace of ancient Egypt, the powerful Egypt that existed as a seat of learning and a source of inspiration to the Greeks who followed in their wake. Although the lay person may not understand the artists' technical approach, the dedication to honesty in the portrayal of the characters, their clothing, and the setting in which they functioned and the grandeur of the period is clearly visible. One feels the texture of the robes. One senses the gigantic size of the temple gods and the strength of the supporting palace columns. The Dillons have taken care to give individuality to the faces of each of the characters in the panorama of people who are a part of this tragic drama. As if this were not enough, the Dillons' creativity extends to the friezes across the top of the page—a pageant of Egyptian personages that give visualization to the text. The depth of research in which the Dillons immersed themselves is a tribute to their concern about providing an accurate picture of the dignity of an ancient and learned people. *Aïda* is the story of warring factions, a story of unrequited love and, finally, the fatal price of loyalty. *Aïda* is a book that will be opened over and over, and each time the viewer will enjoy a new artistic experience.

PROFILE

A Conversation with Jerry Pinkney

Jerry Pinkney has gained continual recognition as a fine artist, a master painter, and a person dedicated to the cause of more meaningful relationships between people of all races and cultures. His belief and philosophy are seen in his art and in his words. Pinkney's words are representative of the spirit and dedication of all recipients of the Coretta Scott King Award for illustrations. Darwin Henderson and Anthony Manna conducted the interview below.

As an artist who illustrates books, what are you trying to achieve?

It's communication. The main thing is that my books reach *people.* People put books on a shelf and then later pull them off when they need them. That kind of longevity is an element of publishing that is the most exciting thing for me as an illustrator. *Yagua Days,* for example, was out of print for ten years, but recently it was brought back to life by "Reading Rainbow," and now it's being made available to an even larger audience than when it was first published. There are some selfish reasons working here, too, since the books I've done give me something I look back on. I can see my growth and I know I have used my art to contribute something to others as well as to myself.

How do you work with a manuscript once you have decided to accept an assignment?

That varies from publisher to publisher. Initially, I do some drawings on a yellow legal pad. This frees me up quite a bit in the beginning when I'm doing a fresh reading of the manuscript in order to get a sense of the pacing of the story. Sometimes I have to sacrifice situations in the manuscript that I really want to illustrate to situations that are going to make the book a better package. There's always a lot of note taking about my conception of the book. At the same time I do a lot of sketching, and sometimes I cut the manuscript up in order to get a sense of which pieces of it will work well on a given page with the illustrations.

How does the use of human models help you to make your characters authentic?

Let me give you an example: I gave the manuscript of *Green Lion* to the drama committee of one of the local churches and asked them to read it and act it out. They acted it out, even painted their faces! Then I photographed them. I

Material in this interview is used with the permission of the editors of *Children's Literature in Education,* the Teaching Tolerance Institute, and artist Jerry Pinkney.

ask my models to read the manuscript and interpret it, and together we find the right mood and expressions.

Can you talk a little about the sense of honesty and integrity that is also so evident in your illustrations?

It is a matter of questioning and finding the right approach. When I first started the sketches for the Uncle Remus stories, the question was "Were we talking about animals or about people?" I was trying to take animals and give them human qualities. That was the wrong approach. But I didn't realize it until I backed off from the stories and saw that they were *animals representing people.* And once again, using the *Tales of Uncle Remus* for an example, I went through my library, which is quite extensive, and saw that a number of them wore hats during the time the Uncle Remus stories were being told, so I put hats on some of the figures. And then I wondered, "How expressive should the hands be?" I caught myself as I said that because I had forgotten that they were paws. So I turned my hand over and mimicked what I thought was the gesture of a paw. So you see, little things like that made me change what I was originally seeing in the stories. And this also influenced me when I was doing the research for this book.

For the Teaching Tolerance Institute, Jerry Pinkney continues conversation with research associate Gabrielle Lyon about his art, not solely concerned with technique, but also with the philosophy behind his approach to book illustration.

Aside from Little Black Sambo *and the Uncle Remus stories, the children's literature of your generation offered few characters of color. How did you respond, as a child, to the mostly white heroes and heroines?*

I wanted to be Davy Crockett. I didn't know about Bob Lemmons or black cowboys. Then at a certain point I realized that I could not be Davy Crockett. Davy Crockett was white. As a young black child, to have to pull toward the main heroes of the West and know that you're not one of those heroes, that you *can't be* one of those heroes has, I think, had a negative effect. Knowing Bob Lemmons or Nat Love would have made me better able to picture myself in that fantasy.

How do you feel those early experiences influence the books you create today?

Our stories should be universal enough so that they touch all experiences, at the same time breathing into them what is different about the African American culture. Attention has to be paid to color, but we're really trying to make people not see color but character. So it's a real conflict. We're trying to stretch the imaginations of children and at the same time speak about the conditions of today.

The themes you illustrate are universal, but you depict your characters as unique individuals, in highly realistic detail. How did you develop that style?

I got involved with textbooks a number of years ago when people became aware of representing all peoples. A simple way to do this was to take a brown wash and place it over someone's face—or a yellow wash—or whatever. What struck me at the time was how wrong that was—that in doing so, we really weren't seeing that individual person. I wanted black children to really begin to see themselves and all the different shades and shapes and sizes . . . I wanted to show the beauty and the dignity of African American people. In order to do that, *realism* was certainly the vehicle. That concern has grown, so that now I have done books that portray Native Americans as well as Latinos. *I want to bring a sense that each person is a real person for that viewer.*

In addition to creating books, you spend a lot of time visiting schools around the country. What messages are you bringing to young people?

For me, it's the ability to use your imagination, to transcend everyday life and see it as wonderful and magical. I would hope that all children find the magic in books and reading, and I encourage them to "hold on to their dreams."

1990 WINNER

Greenfield, Eloise. *Nathaniel Talking.* Il. **Jan Spivey Gilchrist.** Black Butterfly Children's Press, 1988. unp.

Jan Spivey Gilchrist uses only black-and-white pencil sketches to portray a wide range of emotions—sadness, grief, joy, pensiveness—that are the themes of some of Eloise Greenfield's poems. In "My Daddy," Nathaniel's face shows us he is completely at one with his father's music and secure in his father's love for him. Nathaniel says, "He ain't never been on TV, but to me he's a big star." There is sadness in Nathaniel's face as he sits in his room, thinking about his mama who died last year. But one perceives a source of comfort in the shadowed figure of the father entering his son's room. Pictures in close harmony with the words demonstrate the artist's sensitivity as she depicts events in the life of the spunky Nathaniel and his friends. Gilchrist clearly understands all the nuances in Greenfield's poetry and interprets the poems with clarity and a warmness of spirit.

HONOR

San Souci, Robert D., reteller. *The Talking Eggs.* Il. **Jerry Pinkney.** Dial, 1989. unp.

A Creole folktale from the U.S. southern oral tradition, *The Talking Eggs* features two sisters: a favored, spoiled, and lazy girl named Rose and a generous, kind, and hard-working girl named Blanche. The girls are given identical tasks by a mysterious woman in the woods, and Blanche is rewarded for her trust and obedience. This beautifully designed and printed version of a folktale previously known to many in its Anglo-European variant features African American characters wonderfully realized by Jerry Pinkney. His drawing and painting show fresh observations of people and of the animal world. They embody a richness of detail and motion that is harmonious with the tale's idiom, time, and place. In addition to being a Coretta Scott King honor book, *The Talking Eggs* was a Caldecott honor book.

1 9 8 9   WINNER

McKissack, Patricia C. *Mirandy and Brother Wind*. Il. **Jerry Pinkney**. Knopf,
    1988. unp.

Mirandy overlooks her obvious partner for her first cakewalk after she
brags that she will be accompanied by the wind himself and sets out to catch her
partner. The engaging full-color paintings are filled with historical details of
African American life in the rural South at the turn of the century. They perfectly interpret and enhance the light-hearted exuberance inherent in the story
and memorably characterize the pride, self-confidence, and determination of
Mirandy.

HONOR

Stolz, Mary. *Storm in the Night*. Il. **Pat Cummings**. HarperCollins, 1988. unp.

Grandfather's lively recollections about his own childhood fear of a thun-
derstorm occupies young Thomas's attention during an electrical power failure
and helps the boy overcome his worries. A visual story-within-a-story assists
readers with the flashbacks. Cummings's ability to challenge the eye with color
and perspective is as effective as her poignant portrayal of the African American grandfather and grandson inside their cozy single-family home on a rainy
summer night.

Greenfield, Eloise. *Under the Sunday Tree*. Il. **Mr. Amos Ferguson**. Harper,
    1988. 40 p.

Twenty exquisite paintings introduce children to the artwork of the Ba-
hamian artist, Mr. Amos Ferguson. The playfully vivid paintings, which boldly
depict aspects of life in the Bahamas, have great child appeal. Poet Eloise Greenfield has written poems to accompany every painting, further extending each
painting's mood and meaning.

1 9 8 8   WINNER

Steptoe, John. *Mufaro's Beautiful Daughters: An African Tale*. Il. **John Steptoe**.
    Lothrop, 1987. unp.

Two beautiful sisters—one vain, the other kind—compete for the king's attention when he announces he is looking for a wife. Brilliant full-color paintings illustrate the classic tale of just rewards. The artist skillfully uses light and
color to give emotional power to illustrations that richly detail the natural
beauty of a specific region in Zimbabwe.

HONOR

Langstaff, John, comp. *What a Morning! The Christmas Story in Black Spirituals*. Il. **Ashley Bryan.** Margaret K. McElderry/Macmillan, 1987. unp.

The Christmas story is told through a chronological arrangement of five
African American spirituals, lavishly illustrated by brilliant tempera paintings.
Brief biblical quotes accompanying each of the spirituals provide a religious
context, while Bryan's shining iconographic portraits of a black Nativity provide a historical, geographical, and emotional context.

Rohmer, Harriet, Octavio Chow, and Morris Vidaure. *The Invisible Hunters: A Legend from the Miskito Indians of Nicaragua. Los Cazadores Invisibles: Una Leyenda de los Indios Miskitos de Nicaragua.* Il. **JoeSam.** Children's Book Press, 1987. 32 p.

An early Central American legend tells of the ultimate price of greed as well as the tragedy of deceiving one's own people. Themes concerning colonialism are developed in colorful, unique paper constructions and collages.

1987 WINNER

Dragonwagon, Crescent. *Half a Moon and One Whole Star.* Il. **Jerry Pinkney.** Macmillan, 1986. unp.

Half a Moon and One Whole Star is a lullaby that invites the reader to share in the safety of untroubled sleep. It is the song of man and of creature and their different activities as the sun goes down. It is as if Pinkney was an unseen observer in the actions of each character in this gentle story. One sees the brightly colored parrots "rest in jungles deep." And at the same time Pinkney takes you with him to see "Johnny with his saxophone" standing against an early night sky, Johnny who will play at the club at night. And while the activities are either stopping or starting, with mood-setting colors the illustrator introduces you to the child who at the end of the day is lulled to untroubled sleep. In a blend of words and pictures the reader, too, can sing of the night that is marked with *Half a Moon and One Whole Star.*

HONOR

Bryan, Ashley. *Lion and the Ostrich Chicks and Other African Folk Tales.* Il. **Ashley Bryan.** Atheneum, 1986. 87 p.

Using his special talent for blending rhythmic word patterns with all the details of a well-told story, Bryan has adapted a diverse collection of African tales that beg to be read aloud. Through his research into the history and culture of several tribes, this author/illustrator found the roots of the stories in many geographical regions and in his inimitable writing style retold the tales for young readers. As the complete scholar that he is, Bryan included a bibliography, listing the source of each of the stories in the book.

One cannot miss the folktale concept of the triumph of good over evil whether it is the title story, in which the lion tries to claim the ostrich chicks as his own, or a telling of how the born-foolish boy outwits the trickster Ananse.

Bryan extends the text with his own art prints in sharp black-and-white figures or illustrations using the earth colors of the land in which these tales are set. The Coretta Scott King Award jury enjoyed both the humor and the "lessons" in *The Lion and the Ostrich Chicks.*

Cummings, Pat. *C.L.O.U.D.S.* Il. **Pat Cummings.** Lothrop, 1986. unp.

In a flight of fancy Cummings lets readers share in an imaginary trip to an artist's studio where the painter hopes to see exciting new colors spring from his palette. Chuku is a painter for *Creative Lights Opticals and Unusual Designs in the Sky.* His excitement about a new assignment fades when he is sent to paint the sky over New York City and to produce rigid and realistic interpretations. But his creativity was not to be thwarted. Each day he draws sky pictures in unusual colors and intriguing cloud shapes. There are Lovely Light Lavender sunsets, Cloud-Lining Silver and Unbelievingly Brilliant Gold! The cloud shapes take the form of tigers, giraffes, and birds, all of which were done especially for a little girl, Chrissy, the only one in New York who ever seemed to look *up*.

But all readers who see Chuku's figures in *C.L.O.U.D.S.* will find themselves looking for colorful skies in New York and elsewhere. They may even look for a real Chuku who is a very purple young man.

1986 WINNER

Flournoy, Valerie. *The Patchwork Quilt.* Il. **Jerry Pinkney**. Dial, 1985. unp.

The Patchwork Quilt is a story of family unity. In this story parents care, children are loved, and a grandmother is a loving and integral part of the household. Each member of the family contributes a memorable piece of clothing to the patchwork quilt, which symbolically bonds the family. Jerry Pinkney saw all these elements in the text and gave his personal artistic interpretation to the story and its characters. In the colorful quilt one sees a variety of textures, shapes, and forms. This same concept extends itself to the characterization of the family members. Pinkney captures the nuances of skin color, the individual hair styles, and the personal choice of dress. This care for making each one an individual speaks to the artist's philosophy of making sure those who see his art realize that the beauty of the African American is as varied as the people who make up this culture. The artwork in *The Patchwork Quilt* invites readers to visit a cross-generational African American family living in harmony in a home that celebrates togetherness.

HONOR

Hamilton, Virginia. *The People Could Fly: American Black Folktales.* Ils. **Leo Dillon and Diane Dillon.** Knopf, 1985. 178 p.

Forty stunning, stylized black-and-white illustrations accompany Virginia Hamilton's retellings of African American folktales, echoing the dignity of the text by extending each tale's distinctive mood. The harmony of all book-design elements provides a handsome presentation of stories for families to share, scholars to study, and individuals of all ages and backgrounds to enjoy.

1984 WINNER

Walter, Mildred Pitts. *My Mama Needs Me.* Il. **Pat Cummings.** Lothrop, 1983. unp.

Walter's simple text describes a universal dilemma—the concern and discomfort of the older child when a new baby comes home—and Cummings gives visual interpretation to the concept. She chooses mainly mocha brown for the family figures while the use of other colors gives the story a multicultural setting, thus extending the universality of the concept. For some observers an outstanding feature of the illustrations can be seen in the expressive eyes of the troubled Jason—eyes that show the perplexity of wanting to be needed yet seeming to be rejected. There is a visual sense of family, of love and tenderness, when Jason shares the mother's nursing moments and learns to "rub the baby's ear" to make it want to suckle more and when he is asked to help bathe the baby. From a sense of being an outsider to the assurance that his Mama needs him—Cummings's bright colors and decorative designs have captured the joy of this family story.

1 9 8 3   WINNER

Magubane, Peter. *Black Child.* Photo. **Peter Magubane.** Knopf, 1982. 102 p.

A stream of emotions ran through the jury—surprise, horror, excitement, distress, anger, and occasionally a sense of hope. It was the Coretta Scott King jury together examining Peter Magubane's *Black Child.*

Taking advantage of the sharp contrasts that are best captured in black-and-white photography, photojournalist Magubane has shown the disparate world of South Africa through the eyes of its black children. The pictures tell stories of deplorable working conditions where teenagers who should be enjoying life were sweating in the maize fields of Delmas and who return at day's end to windowless dormitories for restless sleep. One wondered about the future of the skinny-legged barefoot boy begging a few coins from a well-dressed white woman on a street in Johannesburg. As a tribute to the human spirit, Magubane photographed a youth making joyful music on a homemade guitar. The book closes with a dramatic picture of the grave of Hector Peterson—the thirteen-year-old who was the first to die in the Soweto riots.

There seems to be a special message in the selection of solid black end papers with which this powerful photo documentary opens and closes. For the many messages in the book, Magubane received the Coretta Scott King Award for illustrations. His "acceptance speech" was a series of slides sent from South Africa and presented in absentia at the award breakfast.

HONOR

Bryan, Ashley. *I'm Going to Sing: Black American Spirituals.* Il. **Ashley Bryan.** v. 2. Atheneum, 1982. 53 p.

Bryan has spent many hours in the research of African American history in subject areas from folklore and legend to poetry and music. With a concern for making spirituals accessible and meaningful to young people, he designed and illustrated this second volume using woodblock images reflecting the "spirit of the early religious woodblock books." With special skill, Bryan includes facial expressions and depictions of body movements in the pictures to reflect the mood of each of the songs—which range from hopeful, to longing, to joyful and triumphant. In what the artist describes as a desire for "visual unity," with what must have been a technique that required unbelievable patience, he carved the notes using the same woodblock style as the illustrations. The Coretta Scott King jury was impressed not only with the words and music, but also with the fact that the notes all had to be cut in reverse so that when printed they would come out correctly! In selecting this title for illustration honors the committee agreed that now more young people were surely . . . *going to sing.*

Caines, Jeannette. *Just Us Women.* Il. **Pat Cummings.** HarperCollins, 1982. 32 p.

The text is simple and very positively feminine. Aunt Martha is taking her young niece to North Carolina in her new convertible. The trip is to be made with "No boys and no men, just us women." Cummings captures the joy of the trip in two-tone color illustrations that extend the text. One sees a small picture of shoe boxes overflowing with lunch goodies; a double spread shows the fun of roadside shopping; a background of moon and stars completes the picture when the travelers decide to "have breakfast at night." The warmth of companionship is undeniable when at the end of the trip the two "women," with arms around each other, approach the relatives' home at the end of a joyous journey. *Just Us Women* is a rich and positive concept interpreted with artistic skill.

Adoff, Arnold. *All the Colors of the Race.* Il. **John Steptoe.** Lothrop, 1982. 56 p.

Distinguished brown-tone paintings provide the perfect accompaniment to Adoff's free-form poems written from the point of view of a girl born of parents of different ethnic backgrounds—one white, one African American. Steptoe's expressionistic portraits capture the many moods of a young girl searching for identity, respect, and security as she struggles to assert herself in a sometimes-hostile world.

1982 WINNER

Diop, Birago. Trans. and adapted by Rosa Guy. *Mama Crocodile. Maman-Caiman.* Il. **John Steptoe.** Delacorte, 1981. 32 p. (New edition: *Mama Crocodile: An Uncle Amadou Tale from Senegal.* Delacorte, 1982. 32 p.)

When Mother Crocodile warns her children to swim away, they close their ears. Only later, when it's almost too late, do they realize the truth in her words. Steptoe's breathtaking abstract illustrations are appropriately presented in a spectrum of underwater colors to create a strong sense of place while at the same time allowing for interpretation of symbolic history in this cautionary Ovolof tale from West Africa.

HONOR

Greenfield, Eloise. *Daydreamers.* Il. **Tom Feelings.** Dial, 1981. unp.

To "read" *Daydreamers* is to first study closely the faces of the children brought sensitively to life by the artist Feelings. Chocolate brown, charcoal gray, and sepia outlined figures of children speak determination, self-confidence, and a strong feeling that they are a part of the future. There is a message in the set of the jaw of some of the young men remembering their history and "drawing strength from the spirit of their ancestors."

Is it the placement of hand of hips that shouts, "I am somebody"? One wonders what thoughts are going through the mind of the toddler pensively sucking on a tiny finger. A study of the eyes of some of the children—eyes looking into the future—seems to reflect Greenfield's words, "daydreamers letting the world dizzy itself without them. . . ." From toddler to young adult, Feelings's illustrations proclaim that "dreaming has made them new."

Feelings's illustrations have more than an aesthetic visual impact. There is a message of ethnic pride and cultural strength that is totally integrated with Greenfield's poetic text.

1981 WINNER

Bryan, Ashley. *Beat the Story Drum, Pum-Pum.* Il. **Ashley Bryan.** Atheneum, 1980. 70 p.

The striking force of Bryan's lusty woodcut technique had instant appeal for the Coretta Scott King jury that selected this collection of tales based on Nigerian folklore. There is a rhythm in the curve of the animals' bodies that captures the rollicking beat and humor of Bryan's storytelling. Subtle use of a line gives expressions to the faces of the characters in the stories—stories that cover such topics as why the elephant and the bush cow do not get along or a jab at human foibles in the tale of the man who could not keep a wife because he insisted on counting each spoonful of food placed on his plate.

With the serious artist's true concern for "truth," there is a consistency between the setting—the plains of Africa—and the choice of colors. This is particularly discernible in the full-page illustrations that show blends of earth tones—reds, browns, oranges—as one would see in the homeland of these stories.

HONOR

Greenfield, Eloise. *Grandma's Joy.* Il. **Carole Byard.** Philomel, 1980. unp.

Charcoal drawings on cream paper tenderly express Greenfield's story of Rhondy's attempts to cheer her grandmother who is sadly packing their belongings into boxes as they prepare to move away. Remembering the special closeness they have shared since Rhondy was a little baby finally cheers and comforts Grandmama. The expressiveness of the illustrations brings an immediacy and a loving respect for people struggling against difficult times, pulling the reader into the story and championing the strength of family ties that carry us through. The illustrations honestly portray both the sadness of the story and the glow of joy and love that comforts child and adult.

Zaslavsky, Claudia. *Count on Your Fingers African Style.* Il. **Jerry Pinkney.** Crowell, 1980. 32 p.

In an African marketplace, young readers are introduced to a way of counting based on the system used in some areas of that vast continent. Pinkney gives graphic life to the concept through clear, black-and-white illustrations. Even without color one is able to see the marketplace and sense its busyness. And indeed the absence of color makes very clear the position of the fingers and the movements of the hands that distinguish one number from another. A close study of the uncluttered illustrations in this book can serve as a fun-filled participatory introduction to an element of mathematics in another language.

1980 WINNER

Yarbrough, Camille. *Cornrows.* Il. **Carole Byard.** Coward-McCann, 1979. unp.

As a modern-day grandmother and mama braid their children's hair in cornrows, the three generations share the stories of the braid patterns that are a part of their African heritage. The charcoal drawings with swirling shapes and dramatic closeups present a series of visions, taking the reader to Africa and then presenting a series of distinct portraits of famous black Americans. Shifting from masks and drums to Malcolm X and Rosa Parks, the drawings soften or become crisp as needed. The illustrations of the African carvings impart solidity, while the drawings depicting the joy of dancing flutter with movement. In the series of portraits of leaders and heroes of black America, each person is easily recognizable and appropriately presented. They include Langston Hughes, Malcolm X, and Marian Anderson. No stilted copies of studio portraits here, but vivid people joyous and proudly leading their kin—the very family glorying in their heritage, in the ordinary world of home, storytelling, and braiding cornrows.

1979 WINNER

Grimes, Nikki. *Somethings on My Mind.* Il. **Tom Feelings.** Dial, 1978. unp.

Tom Feelings captures the essence of Nikki Grimes's "words" in the faces and body language of the inner-city children of whom she writes. The words are often poignant, speaking of the need to belong, the wish to understand "the secrets grownups share," or just to understand grownups. Feelings's charcoal and sepia drawings leave no doubt in the reader's mind of the message of each piece. There is quiet puzzlement on the face of the young lady, for example, who tries to understand the dichotomy of the mother who urges her to hurry into her Sunday best to go to the Lord's house and then emits some telling curses when she bangs her toe! "Why," asks the child, "instead of going to the Lord's house, don't we invite him to visit ours?" Feelings's line drawings are deceptively simple. The beauty of African American features shows in the faces of each of the children portrayed in this thought-provoking collection.

1974 WINNER

Mathis, Sharon Bell. *Ray Charles.* Il. **George Ford.** Crowell, 1973. 32 p.

When Ford did the illustrations for Mathis's *Ray Charles*, little did he know he would be a part of history! Indeed, the drawings in this young reader's biography made Ford the very first illustrator to receive the coveted Coretta Scott King Award plaque and an honorarium.

Ford expresses the joy of Ray Charles's music beginning with the very cover picture—a smiling musician with swaying dancers reflected in his dark glasses. Looking at black-and-white sketches, interspersed with yellow-toned figures, one can follow the talented pianist from his early days when he lost his sight, through the school where he learned to write down his own musical notations, and on to scenes of large audiences enjoying the sounds of spirituals, blues, and jazz.

New Talent Awards

1 9 9 9   **WINNERS**

Flake, Sharon G. *The Skin I'm In.* Hyperion, 1998. 171 p.

Maleeka Madison begins seventh grade determined to "fit in." She has grown weary of being teased by her classmates for her poorly constructed, homemade clothes and her physical appearance, particularly her dark skin. She decides to become part of the inner circle of Charlese, "the baddest thing in this school," even going so far as to change into Charlese's old clothes in the girl's bathroom. She endures cruel treatment from Charlese and her friends, still believing that better than to be without friends. When she sees her new English teacher, Miss Saunders, she is shocked at her face, which "looks like someone threw a hot pot of something on it. . . ." Despite that fact, Miss Saunders appears confident and unruffled by the students' reaction. Miss Saunders recognizes a kindred spirit in Maleeka and encourages her writing skills even as Maleeka attempts to hide her strong academic abilities.

First-time novelist Flake has produced a thoughtful and timely story that explores peer pressure as well as the role that color plays in the body image of African American teens. Maleeka is a strong protagonist, struggling with becoming comfortable with who she is. The voices of the characters ring true and school and community settings are presented with authenticity.

From *The Skin I'm In*

Then Miss Saunders comes over to my desk and stares down at me. "It takes a long time to accept yourself for who you are. To see the poetry in your walk . . . to look in the mirror and like what you see, even when it doesn't look like anybody else's idea of beauty."

—Sharon G. Flake

Chocolate, Debbi. *The Piano Man.* Il. **Eric Velasquez.** Walker, 1998. 32 p.

In this intergenerational story, a young girl tells, with great affection, the story of her grandfather, a musician who played the piano for many years. His love for music carried him from silent movies to vaudeville and finally to legitimate theater. When the opportunities for performing were no longer there, he tuned pianos for a living, always passing on his love for music from era to era to his daughter and granddaughter.

Eric Velasquez's spirited paintings engage the reader and add life to the story. His clever illustrations begin with the closed curtain on the endpaper of the front cover and move to an open curtain on the title page! The animation in the faces transmits the exuberance the characters feel. Color choice is strong, and the effective use of light balances the many warm shades of brown.

1 9 9 7 WINNER

Southgate, Martha. *Another Way to Dance.* Delacorte, 1996. 179 p.

Fourteen-year-old Vicki Harris imagines that someday she will have an opportunity to meet the dancer of her dreams, Mikhail Baryshnikov. This young ballerina is his greatest fan. She says, "I love him more than anything in the world." When Vicki is accepted into the prestigious summer program of the New York School of American Ballet, she is thrilled and frightened. The competition and racial tensions are easier to bear with her new-found friend and classmate, Stacey, the only other African American enrolled that summer. Summer also brings romance. Michael of Harlem may not be Mikhail of Latvia, but he, too, has dreams beyond those of flipping burgers. With New York City and the love of ballet as a backdrop, Southgate gives a vivid picture of a thoughtful and talented young woman coming to terms with class, race, and cultural differences. She learns indeed that beyond the world of ballet, there is "another way to dance."

1 9 9 5 WINNER

Draper, Sharon. *Tears of a Tiger.* Atheneum, 1994. 162 p.

The opening words of this page-turner grasp the reader in a gripping story of friendship, irrevocable injury, and death—a relentless story rife with contemporary reality. A newspaper headline screams:

**Teen Basketball Star
Killed in Fiery Crash**

Andrew Jackson, driver of the car and Robert Washington's best friend, finds his life forever changed by this avoidable accident. He closes himself off from a solicitous family, "walks" dazedly through school and studies, and avoids what seems to be useless help from the psychiatrist. And what of the others? Draper takes the reader into the heart and soul of everyone touched by this tragedy: B. J. Carson, who did not drink but feels guilty because he did not try to stop the others on that fateful night; Keisha, the love interest who worries about

Andy's depression; and Andy's little brother Monty, who does not understand Andy's screaming nightmares. Through careful character development, the reader sees how each person works through this tragedy to the very uncompromising conclusion when Andy, unable to forgive or forget, takes his own life. Powerful words, powerful questions are the benchmarks of this hard-hitting young adult novel. One can understand, if perhaps not accept Andy's decision after reading his poetry:

> I cannot see the future
> And I cannot change the past
> But the present is so heavy
> I don't think I'll last.

Selective Biographies

PEARL BAILEY

1918–1990

Pearl Bailey was born in Newport News, Virginia. At the age of four, she moved with her family to Washington, D.C. Her interest in performing on stage began when her brother Bill, a tap dancer, encouraged her to appear in an amateur hour contest at the Palace Theater in Philadelphia at the age of fifteen. A few years later, after winning the amateur contest at the famous New York Apollo Theater, Bailey knew what her life work would be. Her career in show business included a Broadway debut in *St. Louis Woman*, regular appearances at the Village Vanguard, and singing with bands conducted by Cootie Williams and Cab Calloway.

Retiring from show business in 1975, Bailey made several television appearances before her appointment as special adviser to the United States mission of the United Nations. In 1976 her book *Duey's Tale* received the Coretta Scott King Award.

In 1980 Bailey returned to school, attending Georgetown University where she earned a B.A. degree in theology in 1985. Among many honors received, in 1988 Bailey was awarded the Presidential Medal of Freedom by President Ronald Reagan.

JAMES BERRY

1924–

James Berry is known as a distinguished writer of both prose and poetry. Born and raised in a coastal village in Jamaica, West Indies, this award-winning writer now calls England home. He has been honored internationally for writing that is described as "making a great contribution to people of all ages." His interest in multicultural education manifests itself both in his writing and in his personal involvement in programs that focus on this matter. Among his most recent recognitions are the Order of the British Empire, from the United Kingdom, and the 1993 Boston Globe-Horn Book Award for the poignant story of *Ajeemah and His Son* (Harper-Collins).

CLARENCE N. BLAKE

1926–

Born in Cottonplant, Arkansas, Clarence N. Blake grew up in Detroit but spent many years in such far-flung places as Fairbanks, Alaska; Klamath, California; and Ubon, Thailand. His education includes a B.S. from Wayne State University, an M.A. in counseling and guidance from Gonzaga University in Spokane, Washington, and an Ed.D. in adult education from George Washington University. Blake traveled extensively as an Air Force officer, recounting that he had traveled to every state in the United States except Oklahoma and every continent except Africa. When not traveling and teaching, Blake relaxes by playing the mandolin and the piano, fishing, and taking photographs.

The impetus for the *Quiz Book on Black America,* developed with Dr. Donald F. Martin, came from observing the lack of knowledge of black history "on the part of blacks and whites in the United States."

CANDY DAWSON BOYD

1946–

Candy Dawson Boyd was born and raised in Chicago, Illinois. She earned her bachelor's degree at Northeastern and Illinois State universities and a master's degree and Ph.D. from the University of California at Berkeley. She teaches at Saint Mary's College in Moraga, California—the first African American to hold a tenured position at that institution. Boyd was named 1992–93 Professor of the Year at the college; the citation described Boyd as a "gifted and passionate teacher, writer, and colleague."

The themes that one can find in many of Dawson's books reflect her activities with the civil rights movement of the 1960s, her association with Martin Luther King Jr., and her experiences as a field worker in the Southern Christian Leadership Conference.

Boyd's first novel, *A Circle of Gold,* received a Coretta Scott King Award honor recognition. This book was followed by several other novels that speak directly to African American experience for young readers. Boyd lives with her husband, Robert, in San Pablo, California.

ASHLEY BRYAN

1923–

Ashley Bryan was born and raised in New York City in what he describes as a "household crowded with parents, five brothers and sisters, three cousins, 100 birds, and lots of music." In his neighborhood, people shared stories and family experiences, and it is to this that he attributes his unending passion for the written word and for music.

These interests continue to come together in the volumes of work Bryan has produced—volumes of poetry and collections of African American folktales based on research and embellished for telling and laughter. In his books of spirituals and folktales, Bryan states that his goal is to bring to young and old a picturesque, yet accurate interpretation of the rich store of African American history.

Bryan, who majored in philosophy at Columbia University, studied art at Cooper Union Art School in New York. His work reflects his ability to suit the medium to the story—ranging from woodcuts for his early books of spirituals to the earth-toned paintings in his African tales and from the fine-line drawings that capture the joy and mischief in *The Dancing Granny* and *The Cat's Purr* to the colorful tempera paints that set the mood in his later books of spirituals and most recently in the Coretta Scott King Award honor title, *Ashley Bryan's ABC of African American Poetry.*

Bryan, now retired, taught art at Dartmouth College while continuing a schedule of exhibits and lectures in the United States and abroad using his proficiency in many languages to share his stories with myriads of people. In recognition of his contributions to the fields of art, literature, and the humanities, Ashley Bryan was awarded an honorary doctorate in art at Framingham State College (Massachusetts) in 1995, and similar honors at the University of Wisconsin at Madison in 1998. Asley Bryan continues his artwork in his home in Islesford, Maine.

CAROLE BYARD

1942–

PETER PATE

Carole Byard was born in Atlantic City, New Jersey, on July 22, 1942. Her mother died when Byard was very young, and she was raised by her father with the help of a grandmother. Every time art was offered in school Byard would try to take advantage of the opportunity, but she always felt secretive about her own efforts as though her work were something private. During high school a teacher recognized her talent and helped Byard obtain a full-tuition scholarship to an art school in Ohio. Unable to raise the money necessary, she wrote to the school asking if her place could be held until she could earn enough to attend. That dream was never realized, but she did work at a civil service job, enabling her to attend Fleischer Art Memorial in Philadelphia from 1961 to 1963 and then Phoenix School of Design in New York, where she became an instructor. She has also taught for the Studio Museum in Harlem, Metropolitan Museum of Art, New York Foundation for the Arts, Baltimore School of Arts, Maryland

Institute College of Art, and Parsons School of Design. She has had many exhibitions in major and alternative galleries across the country, as well as special commissions. In 1971 Byard was a founding member of the Black Artists Guild. She received a grant from the Ford Motor Company to go to Africa in 1972. The trip to Senegal, Ghana, Ethiopia, and Egypt was a moving experience and a strong influence on her work. Her illustrations of children's books have won many awards since her first Coretta Scott King Award for illustration in 1980 for *Cornrows,* written by Camille Yarbrough.

ALICE CHILDRESS
1920–

Alice Childress—playwright, actress, and essayist—was born in Charleston, South Carolina. At the age of five she was sent to live with her grandmother in Harlem, New York. Childress recalls that her life was poor in terms of money but enriched by love, patience, and her grandmother's appreciation of the arts—a love that she passed on to her young granddaughter. After dropping out of school at an early age, Childress "discovered" the public library. She says that she began then to read at least two books each day.

Childress's writing career began in 1940. By 1943 she moved into acting when she became a part of the American Negro Theater. In 1955 she was the first African American woman to receive an Obie Award for her off-Broadway play, *Trouble in Mind,* that spoke out against the stereotyping of blacks.

As Childress writes she focuses on reaching African American youth and offering them hope in the "struggle to survive in capitalist America." In describing her writing, critics acclaim Childress as a master at her craft—known for deft handling of the language.

Married to Nathan Woodward, Childress now lives on Long Island, New York. She had one daughter who died in 1990.

SHIRLEY CHISHOLM

1924–

Shirley Chisholm, the first African American woman to serve in the U.S. House of Representatives, was born in Brooklyn but spent her early years in Barbados living with her grandparents. She returned to the United States to attend high school, graduated from Brooklyn College in 1946, and earned an M.A. from Columbia University in 1952. Intending to devote her life to early childhood education, she taught nursery school, directed two child care centers, and served as a consultant to the day care division of the New York City Bureau of Child Welfare.

Chisholm's encounters with racism and sexism in college and her interest in community organization inspired her involvement in electoral politics. She served in the New York State Assembly from 1964 to 1968 and was elected to Congress in 1968 from the newly created 12th congressional district in Brooklyn's Bedford Stuyvesant section. Although she was fiercely independent and an outspoken critic of the congressional seniority system, she served on such influential committees as Education and Labor and the Rules Committee. As she had in the state assembly, she pioneered progressive programs to support women and the poor. She championed support for education and urban needs, while attempting to limit expenditures for armaments.

In 1972, Chisholm traveled the country campaigning for the Democratic presidential nomination. She appeared on the ballot in twelve state primaries and received 151 delegate votes at the Democratic convention. Retiring from Congress after serving for fourteen years, she has remained active on the boards of groups that support education, health care, urban concerns, and minority and women's rights. Chisholm now lives in Palm Bay, Florida.

GREGORY CHRISTIE

1971–

Even at the age of five, Gregory Christie was tagged as an artist, an appellation that remained throughout his school years. Born in Plainfield, New Jersey, Christie traveled from there to the prestigious School of Visual Arts in New York, where he graduated with a degree in fine arts. Working as a security guard at the Guggenheim Museum strengthened his appreciation for artists who were not always recognized for their work during their lifetimes. With recognition already given him, he is happily aware that this did not happen to him. Christie has received many accolades for his work, but he values most the response from his parents. "I can tell they're proud. My family has always supported my art. My father exposed me to jazz, classical music, cooking, and reading. My mother put me through school. I can never forget the sacrifices she's made for me. It honestly pushes me to success."

Comparing his own artistic process to learning a second language, Christie explains, "Realism is the base language, the one we use as a tool to comprehend the new language—abstraction, or rather, the way I visualize people and objects." A magnificent example of this visualization is seen in *The Palm of My Heart* for which Christie received a 1997 Coretta Scott King honor award for illustration. When working on a book, Christie finds that an initial piece will act as a "messenger" for the rest of the book, setting the tone, acting as the foundation from which to build. Christie now lives and paints in the historic Fort Greene section of Brooklyn, a city he cites as being a "constant influence."

WIL CLAY

1938–

CHERYL L. FRANKLIN

Wil Clay, born in Bessemer, Alabama, where at Macomber Vocational High School he began his art career in the field of commercial art. Over the years he has studied at the George Vesper School of Art in Boston and at the University of Toledo, where he concentrated on art history and sculpture. During a three-month journey to Cameroon, Africa, he focused on learning about beadwork, painting, and woodworking of the Bamileke and Fulani people and how these art forms related to their tribal festivals and lifestyles. Exhibits of Clay's paintings and sculpture can be found in private collections around the United States, Canada, Cameroon, and Sierra Leone. In downtown Toledo his six-foot bronze-and-steel sculpture of Martin Luther King Jr. entitled "Radiance" was selected as the winner in an international contest sponsored by the Arts Commission of Toledo, Ohio. Clay's illustrations for children's books reveal the joy and humor he feels when painting and sculpting and sharing stories with youthful audiences.

Clay lives in Toledo, Ohio.

LUCILLE CLIFTON

1936–

Lucille Clifton, a native of Depew, New York, has carved a distinguished career in the field of literature by writing for both children and adults. The high quality of her poetry has more than once been recognized by the Pulitzer Award committee, and in 1987 she was one of three finalists. She also has won the Woman of Words Award, was honored by the New York Public Library as Literary Lion 1989, and in 1993 was inducted into the Maryland Women's Hall of Fame. From 1974 to 1985 this talented writer was given the distinction of Poet Laureate of Maryland.

With a major focus in the field of humanities, Clifton has served on Pulitzer Prize juries and has been a jurist for the National Endowment for the Arts and for the Poetry Society of America. In other areas of writing Clifton has written several children's books and has had stories accepted for publication in *Atlantic, Redbook,* and *House and Garden.*

As an educator Clifton has been recognized as the Distinguished Professor of Humanities at St. Mary's College of Maryland where she is presently on the faculty. Other teaching has been at George Washington University and the University of California at Santa Cruz.

Widowed in 1984, Clifton has "six adult children and four grandchildren" and presently calls Maryland home.

FLOYD COOPER

1956–

Floyd Cooper is a native of Tulsa, Oklahoma, where he attended Tulsa Central High School and continued his education earning a bachelor of fine arts degree from the University of Oklahoma at Norman. Early in his art career Cooper worked for an advertising firm and spent time creating illustrations for Hallmark cards in Missouri. Cooper comments that the art that resulted in this field stifled his creative senses. He then moved to the east coast and was introduced to the idea of illustrating children's books. His first illustrations, for Eloise Greenfields's *Grandpa's Face* (1988), were met with high praise from reviewers. *Grandpa's Face* was listed as an ALA Notable Book in 1989.

In reflecting on his feelings about illustrating books for children, Cooper states, "I feel children are in the front line of improving society. I feel children's picture books play a role in counteracting all the violence and other negative images conveyed in the media." In stating the goals he has set for himself as an illustrator, Cooper states, "I want to take the reader on a journey into the story, to get a sense of the smells, the atmosphere, and the emotions conveyed by the characters."

In addition to illustrating the work of others, Cooper has written and illustrated his own first book, *Coming Home: From the Life of Langston Hughes* (Philomel, 1994). Cooper, his wife, Velma, and their two sons make their home in New Jersey.

PAT CUMMINGS

1950–

ALICE NORRIS

Pat Cummings was born in Chicago but as a child in a military family her travels might well let her call the world her home. When frequent moves from school to school precluded making lasting friendships, this talented artist credits her skill with pen, crayons, and imagination as the source of being accepted, even if only temporarily. Those who have met Cummings would be inclined to add—"also her sense of humor." In spite of many moves, Cummings did stay in one area long enough to earn a bachelor's degree from Pratt Institute in 1974.

When Cummings speaks of her art, in the same breath she speaks of the *need* for freedom of imagination, listing as one of her concerns the rigid rules of art she witnesses as she makes school visitations. One can see her putting her philosophy in action in her choice of colors, angles of perspective, and unusual design details. Perhaps this philosophy is most clearly observed in *C.L.O.U.D.S.* with its action in the sky, decidedly different color names, and a protagonist who is believably purple.

Cummings and husband Chuku Lee live in Brooklyn, with a cat named Cash.

CHRISTOPHER PAUL CURTIS

1953–

Christopher Paul Curtis was born in Flint, Michigan, where he completed his high school education. He began his work experience as an employee of Flint's historic Fisher Body Plant #1. His working career consisted of a variety of jobs, and in this atmosphere of change he began an early draft of *The Watsons Go to Birmingham—1963*. While attending the University of Michigan, Curtis won the Avery Hopwood Prize for his writing of some major essays and the Jules Hopwood Prize for the early draft of the Watson family story—his first novel.

Curtis credits his family, particularly his wife, Kaysandra, for the inspiration to make writing his career. He states further that he also finds inspiration in the honesty of young people and their ability to detect, "what rings true or what feels right in a particular piece of writing."

In addition to Coretta Scott King honors, *The Watsons Go to Birmingham—1963* was also a 1996 Newbery honor book and a Young Adult Choice from the International Reading Association. It was listed in selections from the National Council for Social Studies, noted as a *New York Times Book Review* Best Book, and included in *Booklist*'s Top 25 Black History Picks for Youth.

Curtis and his wife have two children, Steven and Cydney.

OSSIE DAVIS

1917–

Ossie Davis was born in Waycross, Georgia. After spending his early years in the South, Davis journeyed north and attended Howard University where he earned a B.A. degree in 1939. An early project in the field of performing arts was his direction of the show *Cotton Comes to Harlem*. In 1978 he completed the authorship of *Purlie Victorious*, which enjoyed a long run on Broadway before touring the United States. For *Purlie Victorious* and other works, Davis was inducted into the NAACP Images Awards Hall of Fame in 1978. By 1970 Davis and his actress wife, Ruby Dee, were deeply involved in the civil rights movement, working hard to continue the work of Dr. Martin Luther King Jr. Awards for his civil rights activities include the 1975 Actors Equity Paul Robeson Citation "for outstanding contributions in both the performing arts and society at large."

They recently co-authored a book entitled *With Ozzie and Ruby: In This Life Together* (Morrow, 1998).

ALEXIS DE VEAUX

1948–

Alexis De Veaux, a native of New York City, is an internationally known poet, playwright, essayist, and short story writer. In this wide range of genres she has published in five languages: English, Spanish, Dutch, Japanese, and Serbo-Croatian. One of her earliest children's books was *Na-ni* published in 1973. Written for older readers was *Don't Explain*, her poetic biography of Billie Holiday written in 1980, for which she received her first Coretta Scott King Award. A second children's book, *An Enchanted Hair Tale* (1987)—a fantasy written in poetry—was once again chosen among the winners of the Coretta Scott King Award and was selected to receive the

Lorraine Hansberry Award for Excellence in African American Children's Literature in 1991. Among the plays produced by this talented writer are *Circles* (1972), *The Tapestry* (1976), *No* (1981), and *Elbow Room* (1987). Many of these productions were seen at off-Broadway theaters, in regional theaters around the United States, and on television. Among the television productions was a documentary: *Motherlands: From Manhattan to Managua to Africa Hand to Hand* (1986). In addition to writing for viewing and listening, De Veaux's name can be seen as a byline in articles, poetry anthologies, short story collections, and such diverse sources as *Essence, Village Voice, Black Feminist Anthology,* and *Buffalo Women's Journal of Law and Social Policy.*

After earning her doctorate in American studies from the State University of New York at Buffalo, De Veaux now serves on the faculty at that university while continuing to juggle a demanding schedule of travel, personal appearances, and, of course, writing.

BABA WAGUÉ DIAKITÉ

1941–

Baba Wagué Diakité was born in Bamako, Mali, on the west coast of Africa. There he grew up drawing and enjoying the traditional stories told by his mother and grandparents. He said that as he heard the stories he could "see trees speak, shrubs move and logs talk, and all things—dogs, elephants, moon, and stars—move and talk like human beings." It is the heritage from these traditional tales that has become the basis of Diakité's approach to his art and painting.

After coming to the United States in 1985, Diakité's art form took a new direction as he began working with clay and painted pottery. He divides his time between his home in Mali and his home in Oregon. When in Mali, he works with members of the community in restoring and decorating their mud homes and continuing to study the art of mud cloth design under his mother's guidance. When in Oregon, he visits schools as an itinerant storyteller (using the name Wagué), organizes his many art exhibits, and, most recently, produced with his artist wife, Roma, a prize-winning video, *Don't Paint Lizards on My House,* a celebration of cultural diversity.

Diakité received a Coretta Scott King honor award for his first picture book—*The Hunterman and the Crocodile.* He and his wife and two daughters live in Portland, Oregon.

DIANE DILLON
1933–

LEO DILLON
1933–

Diane Dillon was born in Glendale, California, the daughter of a classroom teacher father and a pianist mother. She recalls that her mother encouraged her interest in art over her interest in music because "she could not stand to hear me practice!" After high school Diane Dillon studied at Los Angeles City College and then at Skidmore. Her critical study of art forms and techniques was heightened when she attended the Parsons School of Design and the School of Visual Arts in New York from 1954 to 1958. It is virtually impossible to discuss Diane Dillon the artist without discussing her husband, Leo Dillon the artist, since they met and married in 1957.

LEE DILLON

Leo Dillon was born in Brooklyn, New York, the son of parents who migrated to the United States from Trinidad in the West Indies. Leo Dillon credits his earliest interest and inspiration to become an artist to a friend and mentor, Ralph Volman, a native of Trinidad. Volman supplied him not only with materials but with constant encouragement.

After a two-year tour of duty with the United States Navy, Leo Dillon attended the Parsons School of Design from 1953 to 1956 and in 1958 the School of Visual Arts. He worked as an instructor at the School of Visual Arts from 1969 to 1977. It was during his years of study at the Parsons School of Design that he first saw the work of an artist whose skill he admired and determined to surpass: The artist was none other than the person who became his wife in 1957, Diane Dillon.

Leo and Diane Dillon are, indeed, inseparable in the artwork they produce. They balance their techniques, creative ideas, and perspective, so that the finished product is truly a piece from two minds working as one. Their award-winning illustrations have used techniques that range, for example, from woodcuts, to waxed pencil on toned paper, to acetate painting on polished wood.

Together the Dillons have won awards in the United States and abroad, including two successive years of receiving the coveted Caldecott Medal for *Why Mosquitoes Buzz in People's Ears* in 1976 and the African alphabet/information book, *Ashanti to Zulu* in 1977. In their concern to express the "truth" of a culture in their illustrations, the couple has traveled widely to the sites of their themes to capture the flavor and authenticity of the subject matter.

The Dillons' art has been exhibited in the United States at the Brooklyn Museum of Art, the Pentagon, the American Institute of Graphic Arts, and the Museum of Modern Art in New York and abroad at the Bratislava Book Fair. Some of their artwork is a permanent part of the Kerlan Collection at the University of Minnesota.

Leo and Diane Dillon live in Brooklyn with their one son, Lee, who is also an artist, and "two cats who adopted us."

SHARON DRAPER

Sharon Draper, first winner of the New Talent Award (formerly the Genesis Award) in 1995 for *Tears of a Tiger*, states that her writing career was launched by winning a short story contest sponsored by *Ebony* magazine in 1991. The short story, "One Small Torch" developed into the full-length novel, *Forged by Fire*, for which Draper received the 1998 Coretta Scott King Award for its hard-hitting realistic narrative style. The language, subject matter, and tone of this prize-winning entry met Draper's goal of writing "meaningful literature—readable, yet with depth, to speak to today's young people—particularly those labeled reluctant readers."

Draper, a native of Cleveland, Ohio, was educated at Pepperdine University in California and at Miami University in Ohio. She writes of the true-life experiences she witnesses daily as a classroom teacher in the public schools of Cincinnati, Ohio. Not only for her writing, but for her leadership and mentoring skills, this educator was named 1997 National Teacher of the Year.

Draper and her husband, Larry, are the parents of four children. They live in Cincinnati, Ohio, with their daughter, Crystal.

ALFRED DUCKETT

1917–1984

Alfred Duckett was born and raised in New York City. His mother was a housekeeper and his father a Pullman porter. Following high school, Duckett began work as a newspaper boy for the *New York Age*, a Harlem weekly. This job marked the beginning of a career in journalism and reporting that included writing for the *Pittsburgh Courier*, Harlem's *Amsterdam News*, and Johnson Publishing in Chicago. Following service in the U.S. Army during World War II, Duckett returned to school and formally studied journalism at Columbia University. His last job was that of operating his own press agency, handling press releases for such noted clients as Mahalia Jackson, Duke Ellington, and Harry Belafonte.

When asked about his collaboration with Jackie Robinson on the book *I Never Had It Made*, for which he won the 1973 Coretta Scott King Award, Duckett said that he looked upon Robinson as a role model whose story needed to be told from all aspects, not just from the perspective of his heroics on the baseball diamond.

Duckett, described as a pioneer press agent, was the father of one daughter.

MARI EVANS

1923–

Mari Evans was born in Toledo, Ohio. After graduate studies at Toledo University, Evans accepted a position as an instructor in black literature and writer-in-residence at Indiana University and Purdue. From 1971 to 1976 she was an assistant professor teaching black literature at Indiana University in Bloomington. At this time she also produced and directed a television program: "The Black Experience." From 1969 to 1970 Evans was a consultant to the Discovery Grant Program for the National Endowment for the Arts.

Recognized as an outstanding poet, novelist, and essayist, Evans also wrote several children's books. One of the more popular ones was the witty and poetic *Jim Flying High* illustrated by Asley Bryan. Critics describing Evan's writing state that "it subtly interweaves private and public black frustration and dignity with an infectious perception."

WILLIAM J. FAULKNER

1891–1987

William Faulkner might be called a person with a head just full of stories. He was born in 1891 in Society Hill, South Carolina. In his youth, young Faulkner doubted that he would be able to fulfill his educational ambitions. His mother, widowed while the seven children were quite young, had to struggle to keep the family together. But William Faulkner's ambition became known to an itinerant minister—an African prince who helped Faulkner earn his room and board—and his education began to take shape. Starting with training at the Mayesville Educational Institute he went on to earn a doctorate in theology from Chicago Theological Seminary in 1946.

During his long life Faulkner worked with young people in many different capacities and in many parts of the world. He was the first Negro lecturer for the Quaker Schools and student counselor at Fisk University. Faulkner established the first "summer camps for colored boys" in Philadelphia and in Atlanta, where he pastored the First Congregational Church.

Faulkner stated that he had heard stories just about all of his life. Many of the stories in his award-winning *The Days When the Animals Talked* (1977) were learned from a former slave, Simon Brown, a share-cropper who worked on the family homesite.

Up until his death in 1987, Faulkner was continuing scholarly study on African American folklore, including much of the lore of the Edisto and Sea Islanders living off the coast of South Carolina. These people spoke the Gullah language, with which Faulkner was fascinated and academically interested. The study was to be a major publication in the field of African American folklore.

ELTON FAX

1909–1993

Elton Fax was born in Baltimore, Maryland. His educational pursuits included a B.F.A. degree from Syracuse University in 1931 and study in Bellagio, Italy, on a Rockefeller Foundation Research Center grant in 1976.

Fax taught at Claflin College in Orangeburg, South Carolina, and A&T College in Greensboro, North Carolina, before taking a position with the Harlem Art Center in New York City.

With oil as his special medium, Fax has illustrated several children's books including Georgiana Faulkner's Melindy series: *Melindy's Medal* (1945) and *Melindy's Happy Summer* (1949) and Florence Hayes's *Skid* (1948).

Fax lived on Long Island and at one time served as writer-in-residence at the Langston Hughes branch library in the Queens public library system.

TOM FEELINGS

1933–

Artist Tom Feelings was born in Brooklyn, New York. A part of his early education included two years at the School of Visual Arts. He served a stint in the United States Air Force, where he was a staff artist for the graphic division of the Third Air Force. Feelings began drawing his Brooklyn neighbors in the 1950s, but his drive to depict the African American experience took on a new urgency during the turmoil of the civil rights movement.

In 1964 he moved to Ghana, then in the vanguard of the struggles for African independence. Feelings has written that living there for two years as an illustrator for the Government Publishing House "reaffirmed much that was positive that I had deep inside me about black people." He returned to the United States where he began to illustrate children's books. In 1971 he was invited to Guyana to train textbook illustrators in this newly independent country.

Feelings spent the twenty years after his return from Guyana developing his monumental Coretta Scott King Award work, *The Middle Passage: White Ships Black Cargo.* He has also been honored with the Coretta Scott King Award for the illustrations in *Something on My Mind* and *Soul Looks Back in Wonder* and the Brooklyn Arts Award for *Jambo Means Hello.* This work and *Moja Means One* were each selected as Caldecottt honor books, the first two Caldecott honors for a black artist.

Feelings has said of his work, "When I am asked what kind of work I do, my answer is that I am a storyteller in picture form who tries to reflect and interpret the lives and experiences of the people who gave me life." Feelings lives in Columbia, South Carolina, where he teaches at the University of South Carolina while working on a companion title to *The Middle Passage* about slavery in the United States.

CAROL FENNER

1929–

Carol Fenner, the oldest of five children, was born in Almond, New York. Most of her childhood was spent between Brooklyn and rural Connecticut. She recalls the hours of pleasure she spent listening to stories told by her aunt, the noted young-adult author Phyllis Fenner.

Fenner's early ambition was to become a poet, but her writings to the present have been storybooks for young readers, including the 1979 Coretta Scott King Award honor book, *Skates of Uncle Richard.*

AMOS FERGUSON

1922–

Amos Ferguson was born in Exuma, the Bahamas. As a young man he moved to Nassau and took a job polishing furniture to support his family. Ferguson had sketched and drawn since he was a boy but did not attempt painting until he was an adult. He found that he loved making pictures. Today his paintings cover a wide range of subjects.

Ferguson's first one-person show was held at the Wadsworth Atheneum in Hartford, Connecticut, in March 1985, and it traveled for two years across the United States. A thirty-minute documentary made by Connecticut Public Television on Ferguson and his work received an Emmy nomination.

After viewing some of Ferguson's paintings set in his tropical homeland, Eloise Greenfield wrote the lyrical poetry that accompanies the honor winning words and pictures in *Under the Sunday Tree.*

SHARON FLAKE

1955–

Sharon Flake, a native of Philadelphia, Pennsylvania, and a graduate of the University of Pennsylvania, began her writing career with contributions to popular magazines. In 1992 she won the August Wilson Short Story Contest with her submission to the "multicultural enlightenment periodical," *AIM*. Flake was also the winner of a *Highlights for Children* Writer's Conference scholarship.

As an adult, Flake contributes articles and essays to *Essence*, a national woman's periodical, as well as to the local journal, *Pittsburgh Review*.

As a writer, Flake has focused on issues within her African American community, as evidenced by her theme in the New Talent Award-winning title, *The Skin I'm In*, a thesis against stereotyped ideals of beauty and physical perfection. She and her daughter, Brittney Banks, live in Pittsburgh.

GEORGE FORD

1936–

George Ford was born in Brooklyn, New York, but spent his early years in Barbados, West Indies. It was there that his early love for art and illustration was nurtured. Ford remembers that his grandmother "could draw like an angel" and encouraged him in his youthful efforts.

On his return to New York, Ford studied art at such varied centers as the Art Students League, Pratt Institute, the School of Visual Arts, and Cooper Union. He also earned a bachelor of science degree from City College of New York. Exhibits of Ford's work were viewed at the Brooklyn Museum in the 1971 exhibition, "Black Artists in Graphic Communications." While working as an art director in the advertising field, Ford turned his talents to illustrating books for children. For one of his early works he received the very first Coretta Scott King Award for illustrations in 1974 for drawings in Sharon Bell Mathis's *Ray Charles*.

Ford's current focus in illustrating children's books seems to reflect once again the influence of his grandmother: "Her interest in social concerns and in portraying human characters with dignity rubbed off on me." He proudly shares as examples of this philosophy the books he has done for Just Us Books, such as *Bright Eyes, Brown Skin.*

Ford, Bernette, his wife, and their daughter live in Brooklyn.

JAN SPIVEY GILCHRIST

1949–

The artist Jan Spivey Gilchrist was born in Chicago, Illinois. Her graduate education was at Eastern Illinois University where in 1973 she earned a bachelor of science degree in art education. She holds a master's degree in painting from Northern Iowa University, completing her work there in 1979. With an interest in painting that began in early childhood, Gilchrist states as her philosophy, "I wish always to portray a positive and sensitive image for all children, especially the African American children." In keeping with this position, Gilchrist has many times collaborated with the noted poet Eloise Greenfield in producing fine books of poetry and prose that speak with a positive force for and about the African American family.

Gilchrist has won many awards for her paintings including recognition from the National Academic Artists Association and the Du Sable Museum, which is in charge of the Purchase Award.

The Gilchrist family, husband, wife, and two children, live in a suburb of Chicago.

BERRY GORDY SR.

1888–1978

Berry Gordy Sr. was enormously successful as a businessman and a family man. From his birth to his death he was a living example of the level of achievement that is possible when one sets high goals and works to meet them. Berry Gordy Sr. recorded his life story for his children as he approached the ninetieth year of his life. And this exemplary life was not lost on his family, as represented by his son, Berry Gordy Jr. Gordy Jr., one-time Golden Gloves boxer and later the owner of a small record store, made the Gordy name famous to many Americans. As an entrepreneur in Detroit, Gordy Jr. started the recording dynasty known as Motown. From an eight-hundred dollar loan he developed the venture into a $50 million business that launched the musical careers of such greats as Smoky Robinson, the Supremes, Martha and the Vandellas, and the Jackson Five. As a musician himself, Gordy Jr. composed several pieces, one of the most popular being "You Made Me So Very Happy."

LORENZ GRAHAM

1902–1989

Lorenz Graham may well be called a pioneer in any review of African Americans in the world of publishing. He is credited with being the first African American to have a book published by a major publishing house. Nine years after the novel was completed and after many rejections, Follett accepted the manuscript for *South Town,* an outspoken criticism of racism in the South. This was the beginning of many years of writing in a variety of literary genres.

Graham, who was born in New Orleans, Louisiana, received his higher education at the University of California at Los Angeles and the New York School of Social Work.

It appears that some of the themes of Graham's early writing were influenced by hearing the stories told by his minister father. This is reflected in his biblical series *How God Fix Jonah,* written in the language of the natives of Liberia where he served for many years as United States ambassador. Later books were written in protest of racism in the United States. A prolific writer, Graham contributed to the literary field until a few years before his death at age 87. His last work was a biography of John Brown, completed in 1980.

SHIRLEY GRAHAM

1907–1977

Shirley Graham was born in Indianapolis, Indiana, the daughter of a Methodist minister and homemaking mother. She was educated at Oberlin College, where she received both her B.A. and M.A. With highly regarded musical talent, Graham studied further at New York University,

Yale Drama School, and the Sorbonne in Paris, France. She later taught music at both Morgan State and Tennessee State Universities.

Graham recalled that her love of books started early in childhood. She describes books and music as her childhood partners. Out of this partnership, she wrote a children's opera, *Little Black Sambo,* as well as the opera *Tom Tom,* which was performed by the Cleveland Opera Company in 1937.

A review of Graham's writing shows a focus on historical themes, with many of her titles in the field of biography for young readers. In discussing this, Graham said she hoped to inspire young people of minority groups to achieve the same greatness that her heroes did. Certain factors seem to have had a negative effect on Graham's writing career: Because of the controversy concerning Paul Robeson's loyalty to this country, the U.S. State Department in 1953 had all copies of Graham's biography of Robeson withdrawn from the shelves of overseas libraries! Some critics believe, too, that her writing career was shortened by her marriage in 1951 to her mentor and friend, the civil rights activist W. E. B. DuBois, who was often outspoken against the treatment of racial minorities in the United States. Graham and DuBois spent several years in Ghana in the company of political, social, and educational leaders. Among the educators she met was the teacher Julius Nyerere, about whom she wrote in *Julius K. Nyerere: Teacher of Africa,* a 1976 Coretta Scott King Award honor book.

Graham and husband, W. E. B. DuBois, traveled widely in Africa, Russia, and China. It was in Peking, China, that she died in 1977.

ELOISE GREENFIELD

1929–

Born on May 17, 1929, in Parmele, North Carolina, but raised in Washington, D.C., Eloise Little Greenfield has continued to live in the latter city all her life. Her family moved to the D.C. area in 1930, just as the depression was beginning to grip the country. Life was a struggle for the family. They lived with and shared their home with relatives and friends until being accepted to live in Langston Terrace, one of the first housing projects. She was a shy and quiet child, scared of moving. Since everyone was new at Langston that made the newness easier for her. Her family had a whole house (upstairs and down) to themselves, and in the neighborhood a community began to slowly form. This community provided her with a good place to grow up. She studied piano and joined a singing group called the

Langston Harmonettes. Music reverberates in her books and poetry, which have won many awards. Greenfield began to write as a young wife and mother while working at the Patent Office. But it wasn't until 1963 that her first work was published, a poem. Several of her picture books have started out as poetry, yet she has also produced excellent nonfiction and novels. She is a member of the District of Columbia's Black Writer's Workshop and has held positions of leadership with that organization as well as membership in several other writing groups. Sharon Bell Mathis inspired Greenfield to use her artistic talents to help build a collection of literature for children. Greenfield's many books in this field attest to her continuing contribution and dedication to providing the best for today's and future generations of African American children. In 1998 Eloise Greenfield received the Hope S. Dean Award for her body of works. The award is sponsored by the Foundation for Children's Books in Boston.

NIKKI GRIMES

1950–

Nikki Grimes, a native of New York, majored in English and studied African languages at Livingston College, a division of Rutgers University. Following graduation, she was the recipient of a Ford Foundation grant that enabled her to spend a year in Tanzania, where she researched and collected African folktales and poetry.

Grimes's interests are many and varied. In the field of journalism she has written numerous articles for *Essence;* as a dramatist, she recently led a performing troupe to many areas of China. Her interest in poetry is evidenced by her presence in many published anthologies for both children and adults. She

JOELLE PETIT ADKINS

has conducted poetry readings and lectures in Russia, Sweden, Tanzania, and Haiti as well as in many cities in the United States.

A talented photographer, Grimes has had her work exhibited in the United States and abroad. Many of her books for children have received national recognition including *Meet Danitra Brown,* a Coretta Scott King honor book in 1995; *Come Sunday,* an ALA Notable Book (1997); and *Malcolm X: A Force for Change,* which was nominated for an NAACP Image Award.

When not traveling, lecturing, or writing, she relaxes with needlework and reading. Grimes makes her home in Los Angeles, California.

VIRGINIA HAMILTON

1936–

RON ROVTAR

Virginia Hamilton was born in Yellow Springs, Ohio, in 1936. Her first book for children, *Zeeley,* was published in 1967. Since that time her books have won every major award accorded to American writers, including the Newbery Medal, the Boston Globe-Horn Book Award, the National Book Award, and the Coretta Scott King Award. She is a critically acclaimed author who is often credited with having raised the standards for excellence in children's fiction, folklore, and biography. In 1992 she received international recognition when she was awarded the Hans Christian Andersen Medal for her lifetime contributions to the world of children's literature, making her the fifth American to have received this prestigious award since its inception in 1958. In addition to her honorary doctorates and outstanding literature awards, Hamilton was chosen in 1995 to receive the prestigious MacArthur Fellowship, the very first children's literature author to receive this "genius" award.

Hamilton and her writer husband, Arnold Adoff, the parents of two children, continue to live in Ohio.

JOYCE HANSEN

1942–

Born October 18, 1942, in New York City, Joyce Hansen attended Pace University and earned her M.A. in English from New York University. Before her retirement, she taught reading and language arts in the New York City public schools.

Hansen's love of books and writing developed at an early age, nurtured by a mother who wanted to be a journalist and her photographer father, the late Austin Hansen, who shared with her the stories of his West Indian boyhood and Harlem youth. From her father's photography, Hansen came to see "the beauty and poetry" in everyday scenes as reflected in her first novels *The Gift Giver, Home Boy,* and *Yellow Bird and Me.* Her works, both fiction and nonfiction, also exemplify her interest in the Civil War and

AUSTIN HANSEN

Reconstruction. Her storytelling skill was recognized by the Coretta Scott King Award committee in 1987 for *Which Way Freedom?*; in 1995 for *The Captive*; in 1998 for *I Thought My Soul Would Rise and Fly: The Diary of Patsy, a Freed Girl*; and in 1999, after continued scholarly research, for *Breaking Ground, Breaking Silence*. Working in partnership with archeologist Gary McGowan, the author documents the history of the Negro burial ground established in New York City during the colonial period.

Now retired, Hansen and her husband live in Columbia, South Carolina.

JAMES HASKINS

1941–

James Haskins was born in Montgomery, Alabama, but most of his schooling was undertaken elsewhere. He attended high school in Boston, Massachusetts. Then he went on to Georgetown University, Washington, D.C., Alabama State University, and the University of New Mexico, receiving degrees from each of these institutions. Early in his career Haskins taught music in the public schools of New York City. Experiences in this venue led to one of his early publications: *Diary of a Public School Teacher* (1969). The success of this publication led to publisher invitations to write books for young people.

GEORGE GRAY

Haskins has written or edited more than one hundred books for children and young adults—all of them nonfiction. Commenting on this approach the author states, "It seems to me that the more you know about the real world, the better off you are, and since there is so much in the real world to talk about, you are better off concentrating on fact rather than fiction." His books for both youth and adults have received acclaim for their careful research and a lucid and understated but straightforward writing style. The author has received many awards and honors for his work related to African American cultural history.

In addition to maintaining a demanding writing schedule, Haskins is a professor of English at the University of Florida at Gainesville. He makes his home in both Gainesville and New York City.

KRISTIN HUNTER

1931–

Kristin Hunter was born in Philadelphia during the depression years but grew up in New Jersey. Both of her parents were in education—her father an elementary school principal and her mother a music teacher. However, after Kristin's birth, because of a strange state statute, her mother was no longer eligible to teach. Hunter thus explains her only-child status as based on economics rather than biology or choice. Hunter attended the University of Pennsylvania where she earned a B.S. degree in education in 1951. However, her writing career had started much earlier than her formal education. At the age of fourteen she was writing a weekly column for the local black newspaper.

Hunter's first novel, *God Bless the Child,* was written in 1964. But the author states that her greatest inspiration for writing came after her return to Philadelphia where she drew her themes from observing the life of the people in the area of South Street. It was in this setting that she wrote her award-winning *Soul Brothers and Sister Lou.* In addition to receiving the Coretta Scott King Award, the book was recognized by the Council on Interracial Books for Children and the National Conference of Christians and Jews and has been translated into the Dutch language.

Hunter is married to photographer John Lattany and continues to live and work in Philadelphia.

JOESAM.

1939–

When one talks to JoeSam., the listener hears his interest in and empathy for underprivileged children. In reading his biographical notes the roots of this feeling become evident. JoeSam. was born and raised in Harlem, New York. In spite of what he describes as a difficult childhood, JoeSam. persevered, and after high school he attended Columbia University and later earned his doctorate in education and psychology from the University of Massachusetts at Amherst.

JoeSam. is described as a mixed-media painter and sculptor. In examining his work one gets a sense of an artist who at times is making serious social commentary. His style has been characterized as independent, using simple elements and bright colors.

The colors, simplicity of elements, and the telling of a story with rhythmically angular lines surely were among the factors that brought Coretta Scott King honor recognition to JoeSam. for the art in *The Invisible Hunters.*

ANGELA JOHNSON

1961–

Angela Johnson is a native of Tuskegee, Alabama. It was here in the setting of a cross-generational family unit that this writer heard stories. Johnson speaks enthusiastically of the influence of the "rich story-telling tradition in the African American culture. It is art, dance, and music all rolled into one. I am lucky to be a part of this proud tradition."

DALE GALGOZY

When asked if the protagonist in *Toning the Sweep,* the 1994 Coretta Scott King Award winner, was someone she knew, Johnson replied, "Emily is a pretty free spirit. There are a few things about her that I see in myself, but it was done unconsciously."

With the close of balloting for 1999, the Coretta Scott King Award jury observed that, for the second time in the history of the award, one person was cited as both a winner and an honor winner. That distinction went to Johnson for the novel *Heaven* (the winner) and the book of free verse, *The Other Side: Shorter Poems* (the honor book).

This young author has served as a VISTA volunteer in Ravenna, Ohio, at the King-Kennedy Center. She now lives in Kent, Ohio, where she attends Kent University, works in the Kent Head Start program, and continues to write books warm with the understanding of very young children.

JUNE JORDAN

1936–

June Jordan was born in Harlem, New York City. Her parents were immigrants from the British West Indies. Jordan attributes her interest in words to religious influences. As a member of the Universal Truth faith she was taught what was almost a mantra: "declare the truth"—believing that this can be done effectively through words.

As her writing career developed, Jordan's major interest was in writing poetry for children because, as she states, "children are the most vulnerable and the most beautiful." One of her early books, *Who Look at Me,* was published after she was commissioned by the Academy of Poets to complete this blend of art and poetry as part of a project started by Milton Meltzer and Langston Hughes. Jordan was asked to fill the void after Hughes's untimely death in 1965.

Jordan attended Barnard College, taught English at City College in New York, Connecticut College, and Sarah Lawrence. With Terri Bush she directed the Voice of the Children Workshop "mainly for black and Puerto Rican children in Brooklyn, New York."

JULIUS LESTER

1939–

Julius Lester was born in St. Louis, Missouri, but grew up in Nashville, Tennessee. It was in Tennessee that he later received a bachelor's degree in English from Fisk University. He grew up hearing stories from his minister father, and this love of story is reflected in such titles as *How Many Spots Does a Leopard Have?* Other topics were chosen as Lester more and more realized the need for sharing with his children and with other children an accurate record of the life and contributions of African Americans. The power of this concept was recognized when in 1969 Lester's *To Be a Slave* was selected as a Newbery honor book. When this imaginative author wrote his interpretation of the Brer Rabbit stories in a language that told these tales with dignity, an important part of literary history was made accessible and acceptable to a much wider audience.

Although best known for his writing, Lester is a well-respected photographer whose works are on permanent exhibit at Howard University. He is also a talented guitarist.

Lester now lives in Amherst, Massachusetts, and teaches Judaic and Near Eastern studies at Amherst College.

E. B. LEWIS

1956–

Lewis comes from a family of artists and, when in elementary school where he was known as the class clown, he was unforgettably ridiculed for saying that he wanted to be a lawyer when he grew up. Apparently, he took the ridicule seriously and, from that point on, study became important to him. In junior high school, he attended classes sponsored by the Temple University School Art League and later studied under the noted painter Charles Wood. In 1975 Lewis enrolled in the Temple University Tyler School of Art, where during his four years of study he majored in graphic design and illustration. It was during these years that he discovered that watercolor was his preferred medium. Following graduation, Lewis taught while freelancing. Not until 1994 did he illustrate his first children's book, *Fire on the Mountain,* by Jane Kurtz. Five years and 18 books later, Lewis became the 1999 Coretta Scott King honor award winner for the handsome watercolor paintings in *The Bat Boy and His Violin.* Currently teaching illustration in Philadelphia, he is a member of the Society of Illustrators in New York City and a member of the Board of Directors of the Philadelphia Watercolor Club. Many of his watercolor paintings are among the permanent collections in the Pew Charitable Trust and First Pennsylvania Bank.

The Lewis family, including two sons, Aaron and Joshua, lives in Folsom, New Jersey.

LESSIE JONES LITTLE

1906–1986

Lessie Jones Little was born in Parmele, North Carolina. The daughter of William Jones and Pattie Francis Ridley Jones, Little recalls long hours working in tobacco fields and hating the lingering pungent smell of the plants. Her education included attendance at Higgs Roanoke Seminary near Parmele where she had in-depth studies in black history. After graduation from high school, Little spent two years at North Carolina State Normal School, then taught elementary subjects in a school in rural North Carolina.

After a move to Washington, D.C., Little worked as a clerk-typist in the United States Surgeon General's Office.

Although always an avid reader, Little's writing career did not take root until she was sixty-seven years old. Her first book, *Child Times,* is a three-generation family story written in collaboration with her author daughter, Eloise Greenfield. This title was selected as a 1979 Boston Globe-Horn Book Award honor book in the nonfiction category.

Little, the mother of five children, died in 1986.

GARY McGOWAN

1961–

Gary McGowan has spent the major part of his professional life in matters concerned with preserving history through the study and documentation of archeological findings. At the present time he is the principal conservator for Cultural Preservation and Restoration, Inc., located in Hackettstown, New Jersey.

Since 1992, McGowan has developed and directed the Foley Square laboratory that focuses on the conservation of cultural material recovered from the eighteenth-century African burial ground in New York City. These initial findings became the subject of a 1999 Coretta Scott King honor book, *Breaking Ground, Breaking Silence,* which he co-authored with Joyce Hansen.

McGowan holds a master's of museum studies with a major in conservation from the State University of New York. He is currently the president of the New York Regional Association for Conservation and has been named a professional associate within the American Institute for Conservation of Historic and Artistic Works.

McGowan lives in Washington Township, New Jersey, with his wife, Alice, and their two children, Adam and Noah.

FREDRICK McKISSACK JR.

1965–

JOSEPH BLOUGH

Fredrick McKissack Jr., a noted journalist, started his writing career as a "stringer" for suburban newspapers in his hometown of St. Louis, Missouri. He says of his first assignment—to cover his high school's homecoming football game: "I thought I was 'Joe Cool,' with my steno pad and pen." From these fledgling beginnings, McKissack moved into writing for an African American newspaper, *St. Louis American,* where he covered topics from politics to art. Working for the *Edwardsville Intelligencer,* in Edwardsville, Illinois, McKissack's reporting experience grew as he covered everything from movies to the flood of 1993. McKissack, formerly a writer and editor of political feature articles for the Progressive Media Project in Madison, Wisconsin, now continues in journalism in Chicago, Illinois, where he lives with his wife, Lisa.

McKissack, the son of noted authors Patricia and Fredrick L. McKissack, co-authored his first book with his mother. *Black Diamond* grew out of a love the mother and son share for the game of baseball, and their admiration and respect for those stalwart members of the early Negro baseball leagues whose story they felt needed to be told to today's youth who take the multicultural ball scene for granted.

PATRICIA C. McKISSACK

1944–

FREDRICK L. McKISSACK

1939–

Patricia and Fred McKissack, both natives of Nashville, Tennessee, have lived and worked in St. Louis, Missouri, since becoming a writing team in 1982.

Patricia McKissack (nee Carwell) was educated at Tennessee State University where she majored in English. Continued study led to a master's degree in children's literature from Webster University. Fred McKissack is also a graduate of Tennessee State University, where the two writers met and married in

1964. One of the major connections in the early days of their getting to know each other was a common love of literature. However, in those early years, this talented writing team's careers were on entirely different tracks. Fredrick McKissack worked as a civil engineer, while Patricia McKissack taught school. However, books were always important—and out of this love for reading grew the observation that there was a need to put history in its proper perspective and to give positive messages to all readers about aspects of the black experience.

As a writing team, the couple have concentrated on bringing to light the productive lives of notable African Americans and writing these biographical and historical books at various reading levels. Patricia reports that "Fred does most of the research and I write it up. . . . Fred fact-checks it and messes around with it . . . and we keep doing that until the text is refined."

Patricia and Fred McKissack have a home office and work on a regular schedule, writing, reading, and completing books while making preparation for travels for research as well as enjoyment. The couple has recently added to their joy—their first grandson.

PETER MAGUBANE

1932–

Peter Magubane was born in Johannesburg, South Africa. His outstanding career as a photographer began when working for the magazine *Drum* and as a staff member for the *Rand Daily Mail*, the Johannesburg newspaper. Over the years he has been recognized as the major black South African news photographer. *Black Child*, for which he won the 1983 Coretta Scott King Award, was a follow-up to the more adult-oriented photographic essay, *Magubane's South Africa*. His photographs were outspoken criticisms against apartheid. Magubane's latest recorded residence is in Dupkloof, in the black township of Soweto, South Africa.

DONALD F. MARTIN

1944–

Donald Martin was born in Baltimore, Maryland. His early education was in North Carolina where he graduated from Dudley High School in 1962. After receiving a master of arts degree from the University of Akron, Ohio, he earned a Ph.D. from Ohio State University in Columbus, Ohio, in 1973.

Martin's interest in sharing learning experiences with young people is one of the motivating factors as he teaches and is involved in administrative duties at the University of North Carolina at Chapel Hill. A concern for extending student knowledge of African American history was a motivating factor in collaborating with Dr. Clarence Blake on *Quiz Book on Black America,* a book of challenging questions and answers on a variety of topics related to black history.

SHARON BELL MATHIS

1937–

Sharon Bell Mathis was born in Atlantic City, New Jersey. Her extensive education includes a bachelor's degree from Morgan State University in Baltimore, Maryland, a master's in library science from Catholic University of America, and a fellowship for further study at Wesleyan University. During her career she has worked as a special education teacher, an instructor in a Washington, D.C., parochial school, writer-in-residence at Howard University, and media specialist at the Friendship Educational Center.

ALEX JONES

During her distinguished writing career, Mathis has been cited for her contributions to *Ebony, Jr.* magazine; for winning the Council on Interracial Books for Children writers' award for the still popular *Teacup Full of Roses* (1982), and for receiving Newbery honors for *The Hundred Penny Box* (1975). Her young-reader's biography of Ray Charles, which was a Coretta Scott King Award winner, marked the first time an illustrator award was given. This went to the artist, George Ford. Mathis's most recent book is *Red Dog,* published by Viking in 1991.

With an endless interest in helping children expand their creativity, Mathis has been a member of the D.C. Black Writers Workshop where she was designated writer-in-charge of the children's literature division. Mathis currently resides just outside Washington, D.C.

MARY E. MEBANE

1933–

Born in 1933 in Durham, North Carolina, Mary Mebane graduated from North Carolina College in 1955. She taught English first at the high school level and then at the college level while she earned her doctorate in American literature from the University of North Carolina. Most of Mebane's writing deals with African American life in the South prior to 1960. She has written poetry and plays and is best known for her *Mary: An Autobiography,* a Coretta Scott King Award honor book. In 1983 she wrote a sequel to it, *Mary, Wayfarer* (Viking).

CHRISTOPHER MYERS

1974–

Christopher Myers is a native New Yorker who was born in Queens. He is a graduate of Brown University, where he majored in American civilization and art semiotics. After graduation he did further study as a participant in the Whitney Museum of American Art's Independent Study Program designed for emerging artists. In addition to illustrating children's books, Myers's current work includes sculpture and installation art.

When asked about those whose art has had an influence on him, Myers lists Romare Bearden, Jacob Lawrence, William H. Johnson, photographer Roy DeCarava and multimedia sculptor and performance artist, David Hammons.

Looking to the future, Myers plans further collaboration with his author father, Walter Dean Myers, as well as writing and illustrating a picture book of his own. He currently resides in Brooklyn, New York.

WALTER DEAN MYERS

1937–

Born in Martinsburg, West Virginia, Walter Dean Myers was informally adopted by family and friends after his mother's death. At age three he moved to Harlem with foster parents. In Harlem he attended plays for children at Columbia University, listened to stories at the local public library, and attended summer Bible school at St. James Church (the church that was to become the first home of the Dance Theater of Harlem). Myers learned stories told by his adoptive father and grandfather. The talented writer describes school as frustrating because of his severe speech problem. However, an understanding teacher observed his talent for writing poetry and short stories and encouraged him to express himself on paper where the "words came out more easily." In spite of this encouragement, Myers dropped out of high school and joined the army on his seventeenth birthday. After a stint in the army he returned to civilian life with few skills, very little formal education, and a passion for writing. While Myers was working as an employment supervisor for the New York State Department of Labor, he wrote his first short work for children, *Where Does the Day Go?* He entered the manuscript in the competition sponsored by the Council on Interracial Books for Children and won. From 1970 to 1977 he was trade-book editor for Bobbs-Merrill publishing company. During this time he expanded a short story into his first young adult novel, *Fast Sam, Cool Clyde, and Stuff,* which won the Coretta Scott King Award and provided an important confirmation of his commitment to writing as a career. Since 1977 he has worked full time as a free-lance writer. In addition to his eight Coretta Scott King awards, Myers has received a Newbery honor book citation for *Somewhere in the Darkness* (1993), two National Endowment of the Arts grants, and a MacDowell fellowship. Myers is also the recipient of the 1994 Margaret A. Edwards Award in recognition of his outstanding contribution to literature for young adults. A most recent recognition has been the Virginia Hamilton Writer's Award in 1997.

JOHN CRAIG

When not writing, Myers finds relaxation as a talented flutist and as a browser through rare bookstores wherever he may be. A skilled photographer, he is noted as a collector of photographic images of African Americans, many of which have found their way into beautiful books with Myers's original poetry.

JOHN NAGENDA

1938–

John Nagenda was born and educated in Uganda. He worked in book publishing until he gave it up to become a full-time free-lance writer in 1965. His short stories, articles, and poetry have been published in Africa, Europe, and the United States. *Mukasa* is his first book for children. He is somewhat fanatical about games and even played cricket for Uganda. He has made his home in England since 1966.

LILLIE PATTERSON

1917–1999

Lillie Patterson was raised by her grandmother in Hilton Head, South Carolina. Patterson states that her grandmother, a singer, gave her a sense of the power of words. As a storyteller Patterson used her command of words in developing educational radio and television programs for children. During a long career in the field of education, Patterson has served as library service specialist and chair of the Elementary School Book Reviewing Committee in the Baltimore public school system.

In her writing career, which started in 1962, Patterson concentrated on creating nonfiction material for young readers, especially simple biographies of noted African Americans. Patterson's name will long be remembered as the first person to win the Coretta Scott King Award (1970) in recognition of her *Dr. Martin Luther King, Jr.: Man of Peace.*

MARGARET PETERS

1936–

Margaret Peters was born in Dayton, Ohio, in 1936. Inspired by her parents to dedicate her life to work in the church and in education, she earned bachelor's and master's degrees and a supervisor's certificate from the University of Dayton. As a high school teacher of English and history, she was troubled by the lack of adequate, accurate information on African American history for young people. The goal of her career from that time onward was to enrich the curriculum with information that children needed about the black experience.

Peters inaugurated after-school classes in black history, became a resource teacher in black history in the Dayton public schools, conducted a weekly radio program on African American culture, and introduced the only course in the Dayton schools that focused on black history. Having retired in June 1993, Peters now volunteers in the schools and continues to write and speak about African American culture. She has served on the board of the Dayton chapter of the Southern Christian Leadership Conference and has chaired the Dr. Martin Luther King Jr. scholarship competition, which has helped twenty-six African American students attend college.

Over the years, Peters has been the recipient of numerous local and national awards for her contributions to education, including the Dr. Carter G. Woodson Book Award from the National Council for the Social Studies and the National Council of Negro Women's Award for Excellence in Teaching. Peters has served on the Executive Council of the Association for the Study of Afro-American Life and History and is still very involved in volunteer work, stressing sharing information on African American history.

JEANNE WHITEHOUSE PETERSON

1939–

Jeanne Whitehouse Peterson was born in Walla Walla, Washington. She earned a B.S. degree from Washington State University before traveling to New York to study at Columbia University. At Columbia she earned a master's degree. After further study Peterson received her Ph.D. in American studies from the University of New Mexico in Albuquerque. Whitehouse taught in public schools and served in Malaysia in the Peace Corps.

DAVID KAMMER

When asked about her writing, the author responded that the urge to write was a part of her for a long time, but writing the book for which she received the Coretta Scott King Award came from the fact that she wanted to write a book about her sister who was deaf.

At this time Whitehouse is a lecturer in children's literature at the University of New Mexico and is also actively concerned with Native American affairs in the New Mexico area. She spends as much time as possible caring for and enjoying her string of horses.

BRIAN PINKNEY

1961–

Brian Pinkney continues to gain wider and wider recognition for his work in the field of children's book illustration. Born and raised in New York, Pinkney studied art at the Philadelphia College of Art where he earned a B.A. in fine arts. After further study at the School of Visual Arts in New York City, he graduated with a master's degree in fine arts. While accepting the value of his formal education, Pinkney credits much of his artistic strength to growing up in a family where creativity was the norm. When evaluating his early works, Pinkney states that he wanted to be "just like my father," the noted illustrator, Jerry Pinkney.

With the ever more distinctive honing of his unique scratchboard technique, Brian Pinkney produced the vibrant and "musical" illustrations for *Duke Ellington: The Piano Prince and His Orchestra*, with text written in "classic jazz talk" by his wife, Andrea Davis Pinkney. For the artwork in this outstanding tribute to the creator of great jazz music, Duke Ellington, Pinkney received the 1999 Coretta Scott King honor award. The book was also named a Caldecott honor book by the ALA Association for Library Service to Children (ALSC).

Among the centers where Pinkney's works have been exhibited are the Schomburg Center for Research in Black Culture and the National Coalition of 100 Black Women Art Show. His illustrations have appeared in publications such as *New York Times Magazine, Woman's Day, Business Tokyo,* and *Ebony.*

Brian Pinkney lives in Brooklyn, New York, with his author-editor wife, Andrea and daughter, Chloe.

JERRY PINKNEY

1939–

Jerry Pinkney describes his world as a "world full of color" reflecting the tints and shades of the people, the activities, and the neighborhood connections that come from growing up in a black community. Out of this philosophical background the artist states as one of his goals to "depict black folks as naturally and with as much respect as possible." In viewing Pinkney's illustrations the characters portray the individuality within a group—in clothes, hairstyle, skin tones, and community backgrounds.

ALAN S. ORLING

Pinkney was born in Philadelphia and studied at the Philadelphia Museum College of Art. Over the years his works have been honored by the Art Director's Show, the American Institute of Graphic Arts, the Council on Interracial Books for Children, and the National Conference of Christians and Jews. In addition to being a three-time winner or honor recipient of the Coretta Scott King Award, Pinkney has also received the Carter G. Woodson Book Award and recognition from the New England Book Show.

If best noted for his book illustration, Pinkney has designed several U.S. postage stamps for the Black Heritage Commemorative Series and later served on the U.S. Postal Service Stamp Advisory Committee. He has also designed many record album covers, and his art has been exhibited in many galleries throughout the United States. Pinkney and his wife Gloria, also a writer in the field of children's literature, live in Croton-on-Hudson, New York.

JAMES RANSOME

1961–

James Ransome was born in Rich Square, North Carolina, where he spent his early years under the guidance and nurturing of a loving grandmother. The illustrator states that he cannot remember when his interest in art began, but he does remember creating his own drawings after viewing the art styles in comic strips and *Mad Magazine.* It was in high school in Bergen, New Jersey, that Ransome began to hone his skills in filmmaking and cinematography. An observant teacher, noticing Ransome's skills in animation, suggested that he take drawing and painting classes, and his interest in art and painting seems to have taken off from the encouragement.

Ransome earned a bachelor of fine arts in illustration from Pratt Institute, Brooklyn, New York. Among the forces that were major influences as Ransome continued to develop as an artist were his introduction in art history to such artists as Mary Cassatt, John Singer Sargent, Winslow Homer, and Edward Degas and his meeting with renowned artist Jerry Pinkney, who lectured and taught senior art illustrations at Pratt. Ransome states, "I had always been given the impression that there were virtually no African American artists, so meeting Jerry Pinkney and discovering his large body of work was very encouraging." A warm relationship between the two artists continues to this day.

Ransome says of his illustrating, "What makes illustrating so exciting is that because each book has a special voice, my approach toward each is different. Whether it be through my choice of palette, design, or perspective, there is always a desire to experiment and explore what makes each book unique."

Ransome, currently a member of the Society of Illustrators, has been named by the Children's Book Council among the seventy-five authors and illustrators everyone should know. His 1994 Coretta Scott King Award honor book, *Uncle Jed's Barber Shop,* was one of the feature stories on the popular children's special television program "Reading Rainbow." His illustrations for *The Creation* won the 1995 Coretta Scott King Award, and the book won an International Board on Books for Young People (IBBY) Award for illustrations that same year.

As his schedules allow, Ransome shares his art talent and his time doing school visitations, where he demonstrates his drawing processes, shows slides of his works in progress, and lets his listeners know how he got into the field of children's book illustrations. Ransome lives in upstate New York with his wife, Lesa, two daughters, Jaime and Maya, and the ever-present Clinton, the family Dalmatian.

FAITH RINGGOLD

1930–

Faith Ringgold was born in New York City and was educated in the schools of upper Harlem. Growing up in Harlem during the depression, her family still saw to it that Faith and her brother and sister enjoyed cultural experiences. As a young child Faith showed artistic ability, and her interest in art was further stimulated by frequent trips to the city's art museums.

Along with the usual academic subjects in high school, Ringgold studied art and continued this study in the school of education at City College of New York, where she earned her bachelor's degree. She spent years teaching art in the city schools, but deep down there was this call to express something more of her African American heritage and to encourage museum curators to give greater exposure to the art of African American women. From flat paintings, the artist moved to soft sculpture, remembering the faces of her family and the people of her Harlem childhood. With time came another change in her technique: picture stories in acrylic on canvas bordered by quilt squares, which told full quilt stories with details that engrossed the viewer in "reading" every story very carefully. This unique art style has brought renown to Ringgold, and she has recently transposed some of her historical quilt stories into picture books for young readers.

Presently Ringgold, living in New Jersey in sight of the George Washington Bridge, divides her time between teaching as a full professor and pursuing her art.

DOROTHY ROBINSON

1929–

Dorothy Robinson was one of the earliest winners of the Coretta Scott King Award for *The Legend of Afri - cania* in 1975. A librarian in the Chicago Public Library system, the author states that she conceived the idea for her book during the civil rights movement of the 1960s. It was one of many books that she believed were needed to help children of the civil rights era understand what was being seen on television and her "way of explaining to them who they were and the beauty of their history as African Americans."

In 1990 this author-librarian founded a program, "The Genie in Every Child," designed to help parents and teachers use books and reading to raise self-esteem.

Robinson was born in Waycross, Georgia, went to college at Fisk University, and earned her master's in library science from Atlanta University. Today she calls Chicago home.

CHARLEMAE ROLLINS

1897–1979

Charlemae Rollins was born in Yazoo, Mississippi, in 1897. Her early childhood was spent in Oklahoma with her grandmother, a former slave. After teaching in Oklahoma, Rollins moved to Chicago where she began her career as a librarian in the public library system. It was the start of an outstanding career as a children's librarian—with programs that moved beyond the traditional story hours and reading guidance activities. In circulating material to the children, she became acutely aware of the shortage of cultural material that spoke positively of the black experience. With this observation, Rollins turned her talents to writing criticisms decrying racial stereotyping and also writing quality biographies about blacks who had made outstanding contributions to American culture while overcoming tremendous obstacles. Rollins was one of the first editors of the National Council of Teachers of English (NCTE) bibliography *Reading*

Ladders of Human Relations, which addressed the recognition of the importance of cultural diversity.

For this pioneer in service for children the awards were many. Rollins was the first black to be given life membership in the American Library Association, after becoming the first black to serve as president of the then Children's Services Division; she earned the American Brotherhood Award of the National Conference of Christians and Jews, the Grolier Foundation Award, and the National Centennial Award, to name a few.

Within the American Library Association, the name Charlemae Rollins has a permanent place in the Association for Library Service to Children through the annual Charlemae Rollins President's Program.

REYNOLD RUFFINS

1930–

Reynold Ruffins was born in New York City and grew up in Queens. His educational background includes attending the High School of Music and Art in Manhattan and Cooper Union. A graphic designer and illustrator for commercial ads and magazines, Ruffins has taught art subjects at the School of Visual Arts and Parsons School of Design in New York City and at the Syracuse University College of Visual and Performing Arts.

Among his many awards, Ruffins has received the Saint-Gaudens Medal, the highest honor given to a Cooper Union alumnus. Ruffins' early activity in the field of illustration was the result of meeting Jane

PETE HILL

Sarnoff at a civil rights protest march in 1976. He collaborated with this writer on at least fourteen books. He is also the illustrator of children's folktales, including Verna Aardema's *Misoso: Once upon a Time Tales from Africa* and *Koi and the Kola Nuts,* an edition of which is available on tape with the story read by Whoopi Goldberg. In 1997 Ruffins received a Coretta Scott King honor award for illustrations in Denizé Lauture's *Running the Road to ABC.*

Ruffins and his wife, Joan, live in Sag Harbor, New York.

SYNTHIA SAINT JAMES

1949–

Synthia Saint James was born in Los Angeles but spent her formative, early childhood years in New York City. She attributes the development of her "creative self" to this New York environment, surrounded by an extended family. She says New York was where she learned to color and to draw and where she sold her first original oil paintings. Now an internationally recognized fine artist, Saint James had her first one-woman exhibit in 1977 and later exhibited in Paris, Canada, Korea, and in several cities in the United States. She has designed cover art for books by such noted authors as Alice Walker, Terry Macmillan, and Iyanla Vanzant. Her distinguished style can be seen on greeting cards (including those for UNICEF), calendars, and T-shirts. In 1997 the United States Postal Service issued the "Kwanzaa" stamp created by Saint James. This talented artist has illustrated six picture books for children including *Neeny Coming, Neeny Going,* for which she received the Coretta Scott King Award honors in 1997. She says of *Neeny Coming, Neeny Going,* "This is a very special story to me. This is not only because I enjoyed researching and painting beautiful Daufuskie Island where the story is set but also because the story deals with issues that changes can create, even among family."

Saint James lives in Los Angeles, California, with her cat, Chisai.

TEREA SHAFFER

1969–

Terea Shaffer is a native of Brooklyn, New York. Her formal art background includes an associate degree in applied science and bachelor of fine arts degree from the Fashion Institute of Technology in New York City. While pursuing her studies, Shaffer was awarded the Howland Clark Quinby honor award from the National Arts Club. Her interests include enjoying music, collecting artwork from various artists in various formats, and art history books.

Shaffer is the illustrator of several children's books in addition to the Coretta Scott King Award honor title, *The Singing Man.* She makes her home in Brooklyn, New York.

ELLEASE SOUTHERLAND

1943–

Ellease Southerland, a native New Yorker, was born in Brooklyn. She attended Queens College and later earned a master's of fine arts degree from Columbia University. Growing up as the oldest of fifteen brothers and sisters in a close-knit family, Southerland recalls a household organized on the religious principles of her minister father. She remembers it, too, as a house filled with music. The author relates that the religious motifs that permeate her first novel, *Let the Lion Eat Straw,* are based loosely on the home life she knew. She also states that the mother figure in the novel is a bittersweet reflection of her mother. A sequel to her first novel, *A Feast of Fools,* appeared in *The Anthology of Contemporary African-American Fiction* (1990).

The major focus of Southerland's writing has been poetry. Her works have been published in several periodicals including *Black World, Massachusetts Review,* and the *Journal of Black Poetry.* The high quality of her work won her the Gwendolyn Brooks Poetry Award in 1972.

Southerland is an adjunct professor at Pace University and lives in Jamaica, New York.

MARTHA SOUTHGATE

1960–

Martha Southgate's early writing career includes eleven years as a journalist for, among others, the *New York Daily News, Essence,* and *Premiere.* After graduating from Smith College with a bachelor of science degree, Southgate continued her studies and received a master of fine arts degree from Goddard College. Her interest in and knowledge of ballet, which she studied as a teenager, is evident in the accurate details of her first novel, *Another Way to Dance.* This emerging author not only received the Genesis Award (renamed the New Talent Award), but her book *Another Way to Dance* was also selected as an ALA *Best Books for Young Adults* and is listed in the 1997 New York Public Library bibliography, *Books for the Teen Age.*

EGAN & CHIN

Southgate, born and raised in Cleveland, Ohio, now lives in New York City with her husband, Jeff Phillips, and son, Nathaniel.

JAVAKA STEPTOE

1974–

Javaka Steptoe, a native New Yorker, was born and raised in Brooklyn. The son of the famous artist and illustrator John Steptoe, he states that he always thought about illustrating children's books. To further his goal, Steptoe studied art and graduated from Cooper Union in New York City. With his personal bent for creativity, Steptoe teaches art to children in the Bedford-Stuyvesant area of Brooklyn. When this talented artist speaks of Brooklyn his eyes light up with infectious pleasure and a love of the place he calls home.

When not seriously involved in an art-related project, Steptoe enjoys reading, roller-blading, and sharing time with his sisters and infant twin nieces.

JOHN STEPTOE

1950–1989

John Steptoe was born in Brooklyn, New York, in 1950. From the time he was an art student in high school, he knew that he wanted to create picture books for African American children. His first book, *Stevie* (Harper, 1969), was published when he was just nineteen, and it met with immediate success when the book was reprinted in its entirety in *Life* magazine, calling this talented young artist to national attention. His early style was often compared to that of French painter Rouault, and through the years his picture books showed the development of a painting style that experimented with abstraction, expressionism, and surrealism. Steptoe's tragic death in 1989 cut short a career filled with vision and promise. In his brief lifetime he won numerous awards and distinctions, including two Caldecott honor awards, the Boston Globe-Horn Book Award, and numerous Coretta Scott King Awards. The legacy John Steptoe left to children and children's literature is perhaps best summed up in a statement he made about his work in 1988: "In my picture books I put all the things I never saw when I was a child."

RUTH ANN STEWART

1942–

Ruth Ann Stewart was born in Chicago. She attended the University of Chicago but completed her studies at Wheaton College in Massachusetts, where she earned a bachelor of arts degree in 1963. After earning a master of science degree from Columbia University in New York, she did further study at Harvard University and, in 1987, at the Kennedy School of Government.

Stewart has served on several advisory boards including the Board of Visitors at the Pittsburgh School of Library and Information Science, the Board of Trustees at Wheaton College, and the District of Columbia Historical Records Advisory Board.

In writing *Portia,* the book for which she won a Coretta Scott King honor award, Stewart stated:

> It was my intention to tell the story in an interesting and lively manner of a woman whose life also provided a previously unknown perspective on an important chapter in African American history. . . . Even though Portia was the daughter of a famous man [Booker T. Washington], her career and personal struggles are common to the stories yet to be written of many black women. . . . It is my hope that this literary shortcoming will be vigorously addressed and there will be many Portias (including a few more of mine) taking their place on shelves of libraries and bookstores in the near future.

Stewart lives in Washington, D.C., and has one daughter.

MILDRED D. TAYLOR

1943–

JACK ACKERMAN

Mildred Taylor was born in 1943 in Jackson, Mississippi, but her father soon moved his young family North because he did not want his daughters to grow up in the segregated South. Taylor showed promise as a writer early on when she won first prize in the Council on Interracial Books for Children contest in 1973 with a fictionalized story from her father's childhood in rural Mississippi. The award-winning manuscript, *Song of the Trees,* was published by Dial in 1975 and became the first in a series of books Taylor would write about the Logan family. It was also awarded the first of many honors she would receive from the Coretta Scott King Award committee. Her second book, *Roll of Thunder, Hear My Cry* (Dial, 1976), won the Newbery Medal, was a National Book Award finalist, was a Boston Globe-Horn Book honor book, and was a Coretta Scott King honor book. She has continued the Logan family saga in subsequent books, firmly establishing herself as one of the premiere writers of American historical fiction for children and adolescents. She focuses almost exclusively on her father's era because she wants to bring to life for contemporary children the importance of the previous generation's experiences and work in laying the groundwork for the civil rights movement of the fifties and sixties.

Taylor makes her home in Boulder, Colorado.

JOYCE CAROL THOMAS

1938–

Joyce Carol Thomas was born in Ponca City, Oklahoma, one of nine children. Among her childhood memories is that of picking cotton in fields near her home. A less backbreaking job came later when she worked as a telephone operator by day while attending night classes at San Jose University in California. At San Jose she earned a bachelor's degree in Spanish. Her master's in education came from Stanford University.

As an educator, Thomas has taught in middle schools, high schools, and universities, including serving as associate professor in the English department at Purdue University. She also taught classes in creative writing at the University of California at Santa Cruz. In addition to her teaching, Thomas has traveled as a lecturer in Africa, Haiti, and the United States.

Thomas has earned several awards and honors for her writing in such diverse genres as poetry, short stories, novels, and plays for both adults and young adults. *Marked by Fire,* one of her earliest novels for young adults, was selected as one of the titles to be included in the American Library Association's Best Books for Young Adults in 1982. This talented author has also received critical acclaim for an anthology of short stories that she edited: *A Gathering of Flowers: Short Stories about Being Young in America* (1990). When asked about her most recent publication, the Coretta Scott King honor book, *Brown Honey in Broomwheat Tea,* Thomas recalls, "In just about all my novels, broomwheat tea is steeped, poured, sipped. When I had a headache or caught chicken pox . . . my mother would go into the weed fields and pick the tea leaves and serve me a steaming cup from the crushed blossoms." Readers of this book of lyrical poetry will take comfort in Thomas's mother's assertion as the tea is being sipped, "Good for what ails you."

Thomas, currently a professor of English at the University of Tennessee, is the mother of four and the grandmother of six. She lives just outside Knoxville, Tennessee.

JANICE MAY UDRY

1928–

Janice May Udry was born in Jacksonville, Illinois, a small town that she describes as earning a place on the map because it was the center for the construction of Ferris wheels. This writer, who wanted to write "ever since I learned how to read," earned a B.S. degree from Northwestern University. After her marriage she moved to Chapel Hill, North Carolina. Some of the ideas for her books came from observing the spontaneous excitement that came from sharing quality picture books with young children. This was most evident when she worked as an assistant in a nursery school. Udry is the author of the 1957 Caldecott-winning book *A Tree Is Nice*. Her book *The Moon Jumpers* was a Caldecott honor book in 1960.

ERIC VELASQUEZ

1961–

Eric Velasquez is a native New Yorker, born in Spanish Harlem. His biography states that his parents on both sides are of Afro-Puerto Rican descent. His interest in art involves "a passion for jazz music and a fascination with the African-American experience in the arts." Although *The Piano Man* is his first entry into children's book illustration, Velasquez has illustrated book jackets for both young people's and adult novels.

Serious research preceded his work in the New Talent Award-winning book, *The Piano Man*. In addition to researching photo references in the Schomberg picture collection at New York Public Library, he studied details in the movie *The Exile* by the African American pioneer filmmaker, Oscar Micheaux.

Eric Velasquez and his wife Deborah make their home in Hartsdale, New York.

MILDRED PITTS WALTER

1922–

Mildred Pitts Walter, born in De Ridder, Louisiana, received her bachelor's degree in English from Southern University in New Orleans. She earned a master's degree in education after studying in California and completing her work at the Antioch extension in Denver. With her educational background, Walter taught school in California, served as a consultant at Western Interstate Commission of Higher Education in Denver, Colorado, and later was a consultant teacher and lecturer at Metro State College.

The writer inside Walter saw her close her teaching career in 1969 to devote all of her time to writing. Her dedication to sharing African American history with young readers can be seen in some of her prize-winning books: *Because We Are*, which takes a provocative look at school integration, and *Mississippi Challenge*, a scholarly study of that state's history from the African American perspective.

Walter has been active in a variety of civil rights movements and involved in pursuits in search of worldwide peace. At the time that she won the Coretta Scott King Award for *Justin and the Best Biscuits in the World*, the award was accepted in absentia because the author was a delegate with a group on a peace mission to Russia. Before her husband's death the couple traveled widely for civil rights causes around the United States and abroad in Africa and China.

Mildred Pitts Walter, the mother of two sons, makes her home in Denver, Colorado.

RITA WILLIAMS-GARCIA

1957–

Rita Williams-Garcia was born in Jamaica, New York and spent her growing years in Seaside, California, and in Georgia. Her writing career began at fourteen when *Highlights for Children* purchased one of her stories. A graduate of Hofstra University, Williams-Garcia continued her education and later earned a master's degree in creative writing from Queens College, New York.

Williams-Garcia's novels are noted for their realistic and compassionate portrayals of contemporary, urban, African American teenagers. The author attests that many of her books are inspired by the young people she met while working with a remedial group. The first title from this experience, *Blue Tights* (1987), was followed by *Fast Talk on a Slow Track* (1991). Her short stories have appeared in the following anthologies: *No Easy Answers,* edited by Donald Gallo; *Twelve Shots: Outstanding Short Stories about Guns,* edited by Harry Mazer; and *Stay True: Short Stories for Strong Girls,* compiled by Marilyn Singer.

In addition to receiving the 1996 Coretta Scott King honor award for *Like Sisters on the Home Front,* this talented writer's works have been included in the American Library Association's *Best Books for Young Adults* and *Quick Picks for Reluctant Young Adult Readers* and the New York Public Library's annual bibliography, *Books for the Teen Age.* She is also the recipient of the PEN/Norma Klein Citation for Children's Literature.

Williams-Garcia is a resident of Queens, New York. When her writing schedule allows, she tells stories and gives book talks to area youth.

KATHLEEN ATKINS WILSON

1950–

Artist Kathleen Wilson grew up in Ypsilanti, Michigan. Her formal art training began at Pepperdine University and the Otis Art Institute in Los Angeles.

Wilson's art reflects her philosophical approach to the subject—that of sharing her heritage through "artistic symbolism." Her major focus is that of using silhouette figures set against luminous backgrounds and of each picture celebrating some aspect of her African American heritage while inviting others to join in the celebration. She uses as her media watercolor, wax crayon, oil, and opaque black, the combination of which results in art that has been described as "magical."

Soft-spoken, serious, yet warm and friendly, Wilson speaks of the spirituality that is the driving force in all that she does. The parents of two children, Kathleen and her business-manager husband now live in Hawthorne, California.

MICHELE WOOD

1964–

RON SEIG PHOTOGRAPHICS

A native of Indianapolis, Indiana, Michele Wood graduated from the American College in Atlanta, Georgia, and continued her studies under the internationally acclaimed sculptor, Lamidi Olande Fakeye, from Nigeria. Her professional career has encompassed working in a variety of art forms. In 1993 she was commissioned to create the "Black History Month Jazz Series" poster which the mayor of Atlanta unveiled in the High Museum of Art. Her 1995 Black History Month commemorative poster was featured on NBC's *Today* show.

i see the rhythm, the 1999 Coretta Scott King Award winner for illustrator, was cited by *Publishers Weekly* and the *San Francisco Chronicle* as one of the "best books of 1998" for both the art and the text written by Toyomi Igus.

Wood's travels include what she terms her "personal journey to the American South," the fruits and lasting influence of which were expressed in the book *Going Back Home* (1997), which was honored with the prestigious American Book Award. In defining her art Wood says, "My art is my way of looking back and documenting my history and of creatively expressing who I am."

She lives and works in Atlanta, Georgia.

JACQUELINE WOODSON

1963–

A.E. GRACE

Jacqueline Woodson was born in Columbus, Ohio, but spent her growing up years in Greenville, South Carolina, and Brooklyn, New York. After college graduation with a bachelor of arts in English, Woodson began a career as a drama therapist working with runaways and homeless children in New York City.

As a child, Woodson's interest in becoming a writer was whetted when she was elected editor of a magazine in the fifth grade. Later, three books convinced her that writing should be her career: *The Bluest Eye* by Toni Morrison, Louise Meriweather's *Daddy Was a Number Runner,* and *Ruby* by Rosa Guy. After reading these titles Woodson realized that "books could be written about people like her—people who were different from the mainstream characters in most novels." In her critically acclaimed writing the author, who describes herself as "strong" and "independent," tackles difficult issues and seeks to change readers' attitudes about racial issues, sexual abuse, sexual orientation, and class tension.

Woodson spends much of her time traveling to schools and talking to young people. She considers this work necessary so that "her readers will be more aware of different types of people and better equipped to effect change when they get older." When not writing or traveling, Woodson relaxes by making scarves and quilts for her friends. The writer lives in Brooklyn, New York.

CONTRIBUTORS

Rita Auerbach, a school librarian in Port Washington, New York, is a member of the Coretta Scott King Task Force who has enjoyed two terms on the award jury. She is the founder and coconvenor of the Association for Library Service to Children Storytelling Discussion Group. She has also served on the Newbery and Caldecott Award committees (ALSC) and is currently a member of ALA Council.

Carol Edwards is the children's services librarian for Sonoma County Library in Santa Rosa, California. Edwards was born in Colorado but remarks that the most exciting part of her life was spent in Botswana, Africa. She is a reviewer for *School Library Journal* and *Five Owls* and has been a staff member of the Cooperative Children's Book Center–University of Wisconsin at Madison. A member of the Coretta Scott King Task Force, Edwards has served two terms on the Coretta Scott King Award jury.

Dorothy Evans is a children's librarian in the Chicago Public Library system. Born and raised in Chicago, Evans has fifty years of service in the Chicago Public Library system and looks forward to many more. An active member of the American Library Association since 1972, her services consist of membership in the Filmstrip, Carnegie Award, and Newbery, Caldecott, and Arbuthnot committees of the Association for Library Service to Children and has been both a member and chair of the Coretta Scott King Award jury.

Kathleen Horning is a staff member and coordinator of special collections for the Cooperative Children's Book Center–University of Wisconsin, Madison. With Ginny Moore Kruse, she coauthored *Multicultural Literature for Children and Young Adults* (v. 1 and 2) and was a contributor to *Multicolored Mirror: Cultural Substance in Literature for Children and Young Adults*. In 1998 Horning, along with Ginny Moore

Kruse and Megan Schleisman, established the Charlotte Zolotow Award to be given annually for the most outstanding words in a picture book for toddlers through age 7. Horning is author of the professional manual *From Cover to Cover.*

Hilda Weeks Kuter is the school media specialist at Carl Sandburg Elementary School in Madison, Wisconsin. She has served on the Newbery, Caldecott, Batchelder, and Notable Films committees for the Association for Library Service to Children and on the Coretta Scott King Award jury. She is an active member of the Coretta Scott King Task Force.

Ann Miller is a graduate of Nova University, Ft. Lauderdale, Florida, where she earned a degree in psychology. She has a master's degree in library science from the School of Library and Information Science–University of South Florida, Tampa. She is currently a branch librarian in the Broward County, Florida, library system. Miller has served on the Coretta Scott King Award jury. She is a respected mentor for librarians entering the field in the Broward County system.

Sandra Payne is a young adult librarian in Staten Island, New York. She has worked in the New York Public Library system for nearly two decades. Payne, who received a master's degree in library science from Long Island University and a master's degree in fine arts from the University of South Florida, is a working artist exhibiting in the New York City area. She has twice been a member of the Coretta Scott King Award jury.

Henrietta M. Smith is Professor Emerita with the School of Library and Information Science–University of South Florida, Tampa, Florida. She continues to teach the youth-oriented courses in the library school's east coast program. Service to ALA includes membership on Newbery, Caldecott, Batchelder, Carnegie, and Notable Film committees and as chair of the Wilder committee. She is a reviewer for *Horn Book Guide* and, with Ginny Moore Kruse, has contributed articles to *Book Links.* Smith has served as chair of the Coretta Scott King Task Force and has been a member of the Award jury. She has edited both editions of *The Coretta Scott King Awards Book.*

Deborah D. Taylor is coordinator of school and student services for the Enoch Pratt Free Library. Taylor is a past president of Young Adult Library Services Association of the American Library Association. She was chair of the 1993 Best Books for Young Adults committee. She was also a member of the 1997 Coretta Scott King Award jury and the 1997 Boston Globe-Horn Book Award committee.

INDEX

INDEX